MASTERING
VIRTUAL SELLING
Orchestrating Sales Success

MASTERING
VIRTUAL SELLING
Orchestrating Sales Success

YUCHUN LEE
CEO and Co-founder, Allego

MARK MAGNACCA
President and Co-founder, Allego

TONY JEARY
The RESULTS Guy™

Clovercroft Publishing

Mastering Virtual Selling

Published by Results Faster Publishing and Allego in association with Clovercroft Publishing, Franklin, Tennessee

Edited by Nonie Jobe

Cover Design by Delin Design

Interior Design by Adept Content Solutions

Printed in the United States of America

978-1-954437-11-1

CONTENTS

LIST OF FIGURES

FOREWORD

M A S T E R I N G
VIRTUAL SELLING
Orchestrating Sales Success

A popular expression is "Predictions are risky, especially about the future." We have now heard countless "new normal" forecasts that simply project behavior during pandemic conditions into the future. What differentiates *Mastering Virtual Selling* is its perspective, realistic assumptions, and insights that benefit salespersons, managers, and executives leading an entire organization.

In any market at any time, the most important thing about selling is buying, and that perspective informs this book's discussion and recommendations. The authors emphasize that good selling is grounded in the ability to craft a relevant and value-added buying experience, and that's true whether you are selling virtually or in person. Their goal is not only to help sellers make better use of new tools but also to help them rethink how they sell in response to omnichannel buying behavior—a trend in place before the pandemic but accelerated by it.

Moreover, the authors do not assume that we're entering a digital-eats-physical world. Buying has always been a social as well as economic transaction. Hence, it's not an either-or choice (virtual versus in person) when it comes to selling. Digital tools were available for years before the pandemic forced firms to use them in go-to-market initiatives. Once used, many companies found that, in effect, they had been overpaying for certain tasks in their sales models, ranging from lead generation and demos to meetings where virtual means can be used productively. As the authors emphasize, while virtual experiences will not "replace our need for true human interaction, virtual selling is here to stay."

Especially in B2B markets, the real need is the integration of virtual selling into hybrid models of interaction with customers. This book explains how to do that by leveraging other resources across the organization in a team-selling model to improve results. Think about the impact to your company of increasing available selling time by 10–20 percent. For most companies, that's not only a major productivity benefit; it also increases the total addressable market because segments that were too costly to reach now become economically feasible.

Finally, *Mastering Virtual Selling* is also a book for managers, not pundits with an abstract understanding of technology but no experience with actual sales management. In business, selling effectiveness is an organizational outcome, not only the result of skilled salespeople in your firm. The theme throughout this book is orchestrating sales success by mobilizing organizational assets and behaviors. Yuchun Lee, Mark Magnacca, and Tony Jeary collectively bring decades of experience to the topic, and their pragmatism and street smarts inform their practical advice. Their distinction between "frontstage" and "backstage" activities is important for managers in all sales models, and they provide useful ways of building the required capabilities while debunking many myths about virtual selling.

In a world where competitors will also be using virtual tools and where buyers are already bombarded with messages through multiple media, the authors note that time is the scarce resource. That scarcity has at least two dimensions that are crucial in sales: the time required to manage the buying cycle and the amount of actual face time (either in person or virtual) with target customers. Their insights about aligning synchronous and asynchronous communications are essential. You can use those insights to improve selling skills, increase required cross-functional collaboration in your company, and allocate training, onboarding, coaching, and other resources more effectively.

The future is never what it used to be but it arrives daily, and it's not the responsibility of the market to adapt to your preferred sales approach. It's your responsibility to adapt to the market. *Mastering Virtual Selling* can help you do that, navigate the thicket of claims made about online technologies, and better use those tools in customer acquisition and retention.

—**Frank V. Cespedes** teaches at Harvard
Business School and is the author of
*Sales Management That Works: How to Sell in a World
That Never Stops Changing*

INTRODUCTION

I n an instant everything flipped! In March 2020 the world turned upside down. People just about everywhere needed to learn a new way to work. And we are betting you were one of them.

Almost 90 percent of selling has moved to a remote model since the COVID-19 pandemic began, according to research from McKinsey, and most B2B companies' products and services are now being sold virtually.[1]

What exactly is **virtual selling**[2]? It's not just a series of Zoom meetings! Zoom is just one new way of communicating with your customers virtually.

Virtual selling is about working a deal remotely when you can't be there in person, and it is the new normal. Learning how to do this effectively is critical to your success.

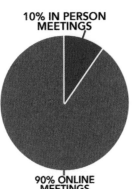

10% IN PERSON MEETINGS

90% ONLINE MEETINGS

"Virtual selling is not a series of Zoom meetings."

Being a great virtual seller means understanding a prospect's mindset when you are not meeting with him/her in person and using all the tools and techniques available to be the most successful. While the universal principles of selling are the same, you have new obstacles to overcome and new skills to master.

That's the challenge. But the opportunity is that there are many advantages in this new normal if you know how to leverage them.

There are three types of people in this world—those who make things happen, those who watch them happen, and those who wonder what happened. **Which kind will you be?**

That's an important question because the mindset you bring to this process will, to a large extent, determine how well you succeed going forward.

WHY READ THIS BOOK?

Mastering virtual selling involves learning a set of insights, disciplines, processes, and technology solutions that equip you to successfully nurture prospects, share information, conduct demos, and host meetings without the benefit of being face-to-face. This book will help improve results for executives, sales leaders, and individual sellers.

We (your coauthors) have worked with tens of thousands of sales professionals around the world and developed unique expertise in virtual selling that can give you an edge. While this book is written primarily for those in B2B (business-to-business) selling, there will be things you can utilize if you are in B2C (business-to-consumer) selling as well.

Everyone in the selling profession is now on a level playing field—we are all, in essence, apprentices! The goal of an apprentice, of course, is to eventually become a **master**. And just as an apprentice trains for mastery by working alongside someone more experienced, we invite you to come alongside the three of us as we share our combined knowledge and experiences to help you become a master virtual seller.

BECOMING A MASTER (OR MORE SPECIFICALLY, A MAESTRO)

Merriam-Webster defines **orchestrate** as *"to arrange or combine so as to achieve a desired or maximum effect."*[3]

The image on the cover reveals the essence of this book, which is learning to be a **maestro** (master) at orchestrating all the moving parts in the buying process to achieve the outcome you want. Having a clear strategy to orchestrate that outcome is what separates average salespeople from the masters of virtual selling.

British American conductor Benjamin Zander, founder and director of the Boston Philharmonic Orchestra, is a truly great maestro. The music he helps his orchestra create exemplifies the power that comes from coordinating a number of different people and activities backstage to create beautiful music frontstage. Similarly, as a maestro of virtual selling you're pulling together many elements of your "backstage" effort—coordinating people and schedules, leveraging resources to help, and sharing key content that will help the buyer's decision-making process while nurturing the relationship and building trust. You're doing all this to create a compelling and effective buying experience to achieve the desired outcome. (In chapter 2, we share how a personal experience with Ben Zander provided the foundation for the authors to synthesize and organize their collective insights in virtual selling into frontstage and backstage activities, which are explained in depth in chapters 3 and 4.)

THE PAYOFF

After reading this book, you (and your team) will understand how to master virtual selling and leverage your most important resource—time. You will know what skills to hone and what new techniques you need to help you become more proficient at virtual selling, and you will be more confident, productive, and on track to becoming a "master."

While some may still be thinking, "The best way to sell is face-to-face" or "Using technology creates a barrier between me and the prospect," you will be moving ahead and leaving the competition behind.

WHO WE ARE

We are entrepreneurs and strategic consultants who have started and grown successful businesses.

Yuchun Lee is an experienced software executive and is well known in the high-tech community as a member of the famous MIT Blackjack Team, portrayed in the film *21*. He cofounded and led the marketing automation software company Unica, which he took public before it was subsequently acquired by IBM. Yuchun is currently the co-founder and CEO of Allego, the leading learning and **sales-enablement** platform for B2B sales teams.

Mark Magnacca has an extensive background and track record of bringing ideas to life. After starting a financial planning company right out of college and selling it a decade later, he then started a sales consulting business to support a wide range of financial services companies as they began their digital transformation. He's the author of *So What? How to Communicate What Really Matters to Your Audience* and *The Product is YOU!* Mark is currently the co-founder and president of Allego.

Tony Jeary, known as The RESULTS Guy™, has written over sixty books—twenty-five about presentation, selling, or communication. His company, Tony Jeary International, has consulted with many of the top companies around the globe, helping them find innovative ways to get the results they want faster. Tony and Mark have been working together over the span of two decades.

Not surprisingly, your authors have been using virtual platforms as part of their businesses for many years, starting well before the pandemic hit. In fact, the entire writing and **collaboration** process of this book was done virtually.

We understand that there must be a new way of thinking regarding virtual selling if sales teams and companies are to survive and thrive going forward. Our goal is to get everyone, everywhere to rethink how they sell.

OUR PROMISE TO YOU

This book will transform your approach to virtual selling. Our highest hope, though, is that you will experience epiphanies—literally life-changing insights—that will help you become a master at virtual selling and improve your sales results if you put these ideas to work.

WHAT'S AHEAD

Being a successful virtual seller demands new proficiencies. This book is the answer to the virtual selling puzzle and will help you and/or your team be the very best you can be. It is organized into these chapters:

Chapter 1: Creating an Exceptional Buying Experience. In this chapter, we outline a basic understanding of *what good selling is* and the difference between your selling cycle and the buying cycle. We share three foundational selling imperatives that are critical to mastering *any* sales situation, including virtual selling.

Chapter 2: The Power of Orchestration. A maestro creates a powerful experience for his audience. We will introduce you in this chapter to a framework for how to consistently create a compelling buying experience for your buyers.

Chapters 3 and 4: Frontstage Selling and **Backstage Selling**, respectively. In these two chapters we will help you learn how to master the realm of

synchronous collaboration, which is "frontstage," and **asynchronous** collaboration, which is "backstage." Plus, we give you the tools you need to build your frontstage and backstage **arsenals** that will serve as templates and reference materials that support your efforts.

Chapter 5: Enabling Virtual Selling Teams. Here we present a framework for sales management and paint a picture of the key sales processes—including leveraging technology, creating and enhancing a team-selling culture, focusing on bringing agility to your team, and leveraging data—to improve and optimize your results.

Chapter 6: Stepping Confidently into the Future. With the shift to a virtual work environment and a hybrid form of selling, it's harder than ever to get in front of the right people, at the right time, with the right message. This book helps you accelerate your understanding about the virtual selling process by giving you the tools, processes, and tactics you need to adjust to the new normal and become a master at virtual selling.

A BONUS FOR YOU

We have included in the Appendix a summary of the book, which can be used as a quick-start guide for those of you who want to quickly understand its key messages. That way, you can either read the book from cover to cover or you can select the chapters that are most relevant to you.

CASE STUDY NO. 1:
IF YOU ARE SKEPTICAL:

Michael exemplified a veteran B2B salesperson. As a perennial top performer for twenty-five years in the pre-pandemic, in-person selling era, Michael was skeptical about whether he should embrace the concept of virtual selling when his company announced a work-from-home policy in March 2020. Although he was fluent with technology, he was not a "digital native" and had seen many of management's "flavors of the week" come and go. He was glad he had not jumped on every new trend that had come down the line, many of which turned out to be unimportant in the long run.

However, one offhand comment from his longtime customer, Tim, caused him to rethink the significance of this profound change in the world of selling. In May of 2020, Michael said to Tim, "I'm really sorry I can't be there in person to help you with the presentation to the larger team," regarding a deal they had collaborated on for seven months. He recounted how they had done this "dog-and-pony show" multiple times together, and they both actually enjoyed it as well as their premeeting dinner to get caught up. Tim paused and said quietly, "Michael, you are helping me. I am going to introduce you to the team, but I need to do everything you would have done in person with less time. In fact, I need you to do a short video for the team to watch before the live virtual meeting because we only have twenty minutes with the full management team, not an hour." In that moment it occurred to Michael that, other than the dinner he missed, he could actually do everything he was going to do in person and more. The management team was a group of busy executives who had many other issues to handle, and they wanted to quickly make a decision about the value of investing in Michael's enterprise software platform during a pandemic. Michael realized he *could* make it a great experience for them. He and Tim completed the presentation, and Tim texted Michael later that day to say, "We just got the green light on this project. Let's get started." Michael had completed this transaction to help his customer buy software they needed to adapt to the virtual selling world, and he had done it all without leaving his house. After this deal closed, Michael decided to go all in on virtual selling, and he had the second best year in his sales career in 2020, despite a global pandemic.

What will it take for you to go all in?

ENDNOTES

1 Ryan Gavin, Liz Harrison, Candace Lun Plotkin, Dennis Spillecke, and Jennifer Stanley, "The B2B Digital Inflection Point: How Sales Have Changed During COVID-19," McKinsey & Company, https://www.mckinsey.com/business-functions/marketing-and-sales/our-insights/the-b2b-digital-inflection-point-how-sales-have-changed-during-covid-19#.

2 Terms defined in the Glossary are boldfaced in red at first appearance.

3 Merriam-Webster.com, https://www.merriam-webster.com/dictionary/orchestrate.

CREATING AN EXCEPTIONAL BUYING EXPERIENCE

chapter 1

"It's not what you don't know that gets you into trouble, it's what you know for sure that ain't so."
— Mark Twain

Mastering virtual selling starts with mastering the art of selling. You will not succeed in virtual selling if you are not good at selling—period! So what follows from this is you need to have a proper command of what good selling is before you can successfully make the transition.

Let's look at a non-selling example to make the point. We can probably all agree that Al Pacino is recognized as a successful movie actor. What you may not know, however, is that Pacino was first a great live-stage actor. Director Francis Ford Coppola saw him on stage and hired him to play Michael Corleone in *The Godfather*, for which he received an Oscar nomination. This shows how someone who excelled in the live, in-person format of the stage went on to become a master in the virtual format of movies.

It's the same with sales. If you have worked hard to master the domain of face-to-face selling, you can transition to virtual selling by leveraging your existing skills and learning new ones.

If you are new to the world of selling, welcome! This is the ideal time to build the right habits to help you succeed in what is likely to become a hybrid model of virtual and in-person B2B selling going forward. In fact, you may be able to catch up quickly with the veterans in your field since much of modern virtual selling is new. **Seasoned sellers, beware—you need to adapt quickly if you want to leverage your tenure.**

WHAT GOOD SELLING IS

Good selling, of course, is grounded in creating an exceptional buying experience. But most salespeople put their emphasis in the wrong place. They tend to focus on the selling cycle versus the buying cycle. But the selling cycle, of course, is all about you and your timeline. The focus is on moving your customer through the steps in your funnel from start to close, which likely includes typical elements such as:

- ▶ generating initial interest;
- ▶ qualifying;
- ▶ demonstrating value;
- ▶ differentiating your product or service;
- ▶ negotiating; and
- ▶ closing the deal.

Notice anything missing? These elements focus only on your needs. They don't address solving your buyer's problem. **Today's buyers don't want to be sold; they want to buy.**

> *Buyers want you to satisfy their needs. It is all about them. Not you.*

Buyers today are concerned about *their needs*, not your process. Successful sellers think about selling as a *service* to the buyer. They have a problem that needs a solution, and they want to make an informed decision—which includes understanding their options and making the right choice while reducing their risk. "Today's buyers control their journey through the buying cycle much more than vendors control the selling cycle. In a recent survey, 74 percent of buyers told us they conduct more than half of their research online before making an offline purchase,"[1] the research firm Forrester wrote.

A buyer's journey includes things like:

- ▶ gaining awareness;
- ▶ identifying problems;
- ▶ finding options for solutions;
- ▶ creating a list of possible providers;
- ▶ negotiating;
- ▶ buying and then implementing their solution.

Successful sellers fuse the selling cycle with the buying cycle so they are two sides of the same coin. So what does an appropriate cycle look like?

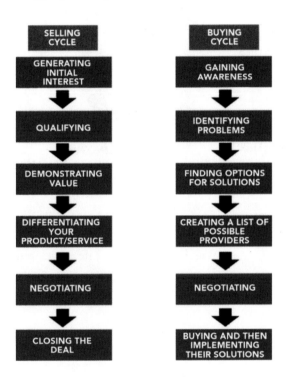

Successful sellers think about selling as a service to the buyer, and they fuse the selling cycle with the buying cycle so they are two sides of the same coin.

The chart that follows from SPARXiQ helps you apply these buyer-centric principles to every sales activity.

MANAGE THE SALES PROCESS

Uncover and meet decision criteria for each buyer at each stage, building trust and gaining commitments throughout.

UNDERSTAND YOUR BUYER

Seek to truly understand your buyer's role in the company, their goals and buying process.

Think **"COIN-OP"** to understand their Challenges, Opportunities, Impacts, Needs, Outcomes, and Priorities.

CO-CREATE SOLUTIONS

Collaborate to configure the best solution, combining your knowledge of your product and your buyer's knowledge of their situation.

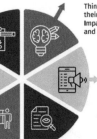

CRAFT TARGETED MESSAGES

Speak directly to the buyer by messaging personalized value and offering solutions to problems.

QUALIFY THE OPPORTUNITY

Ensure you have **N**eed **A**nd **S**olution **A**lignment (**NASA**) and proceed with the **FACTs** in mind: Funding, Alternatives, Committee, and Timing.

UNCOVER WHAT'S VALUABLE

Assess your buyer's current and future state to determine their needs and inform your sales approach.

Managing the sales process. Courtesy of SPARXiQ.com

At the highest level, the goal is to create a harmonious balance between the selling and buying cycles, whether we are talking about in-person sales or virtual sales, and it involves certain imperatives:

1. Researching and building **rapport**—discovering all you can about your buyer and your buyer's organization and building a relationship with them based on trust and genuine interest.

2. Understanding and solving your buyer's problems— listening to your buyers to clearly understand their wants and needs and providing solutions to those needs.

3. Leveraging success—creating a win-win outcome for both the buyer and you and leveraging this experience for future work together.

Let's unpack these imperatives to give you the foundation for good selling that will allow you to move toward mastery.

STEP 1: RESEARCHING AND BUILDING RAPPORT

Curiosity is one of the most valuable traits a person in sales can have. The more curious you are about the buyer and the buyer's company, the more effective research you will do. And the more research you do, the more impressed your buyer will be, as it shows you have a genuine interest in solving the problem at hand.

The most successful salespeople have an innate curiosity, which is one of the most valuable traits a salesperson can have.

There has never been a better time to be a curious person than this early part of the twenty-first century. Never before has so much information been so readily available to so many people—and all for free. Imagine going back in time and explaining to one of the great masters of the past, Leonardo da Vinci, that 500 years in the future people would be able to "tap a piece of glass" and access the most up-to-date knowledge on *virtually any topic* that has ever been studied.

Think how easy it is today for you to answer any question you may have on any topic and do so with just a few taps on your smart phone. Who has not been at a dinner when a question arose and someone pulled out his or her phone and answered the question in ten seconds or less? This may not seem amazing to us because it is so common, but think about how da Vinci would see it.

Da Vinci embodied the Renaissance ideal. He was not only one of the best artists of his time but probably also the greatest inventor ever. He was also a scientist, anatomist, mathematician, sculptor, botanist, musician, author, and even more—and he was largely self-taught! He did all that with little formal schooling. What was his secret? He was *hugely curious*—perhaps one of the most curious persons in history—and he gained inspiration from both nature and the world surrounding him. To paint persons as accurately as possible, he performed anatomical studies that also helped him understand some of the mechanics behind many of his machines.

Never satisfied to look at something from a single angle, he rotated, disassembled, and dissected his object of study to get the utmost understanding of the problems he was wrestling with. *Curiosity fueled the research that helped make da Vinci a "master" in the truest sense of the word.*

In your quest for mastery, there is no substitute for doing extensive research in order to be prepared. Sellers who think they can get by without having a genuine interest in the buyer and the problem to be solved will seldom, if ever, achieve mastery.

The amount of research required for every opportunity will vary; it's up to you to refine your judgment and understand when you need to immerse yourself in the topic or if a topical understanding of the problem or industry is sufficient.

At a minimum, you should research your buyer's LinkedIn profile, Google your contact and his or her company, and study the company's website. Where relevant, you can gain a wealth of useful information by listening to an interview with the CEO or an earnings call for a public company.

If you're operating at the mastery level, though, you will harness the power of your curiosity and take things to a deeper level if the degree of the sale justifies it. For example, when you study your buyer's LinkedIn profile, you can look to see whether you have common connections. If you do, you can contact these people to see what insight you might obtain on the person and perhaps the company. That kind of firsthand knowledge can often be invaluable, and you will have the dual advantage of being able to use those mutual connections when building your relationship with the buyer. The more commonalities you can find, the better. Your buyers will notice and appreciate how prepared you are, and it will help you build rapport faster.

Some salespeople think this is too much, and they are concerned about looking like a stalker. However, based on working with sellers across multiple industries, this is an outdated worldview in a time when virtually all employers use some type of background check and Google search on candidates, and most people going on a first date do the same thing. You do not need to use everything you learn, but if what you are seeking is public anyway, why would you not want to know it?

Think of the reactions when a salesperson shows up—either in person or virtually—clearly ignorant about the industry, company, and prospect. You don't need to be an expert for a first call, but do enough research to show you care. Otherwise, you will be wasting their time and yours asking questions that could be easily answered before the call.

A Good Seller ...	A Bad Seller ...
Sets the stage before a meeting by sending an agenda to clarify the meeting objectives and has LinkedIn profiles printed to be able to call people by name	Thinks he or she can just wing it
Does pre-call research to look for commonality and sends LinkedIn invitations. Ready to ask "good questions" of the buyer	Asks questions that were easily answerable with simple research and does not connect on LinkedIn
Arrives early or on time to allow for a more personal connection	Arrives late
Asks the buyer, "What does success look like to you?" to confirm he or she can actually help	Assumes he or she knows what is important to the buyer
Shares a photo or icon about something he or she has in common with the buyer, such as a school they both attended, and says, "Did you know . . . ?"	Asks questions like an interrogation or obviously to check off a list
Understands how to adapt his or her communication style based on the buyer's communication style (speech rate, volume, etc.)	Uses the same approach with every buyer and expects the buyer to adapt to him or her
Facilitates introductions, discussion, note taking, and action items, and manages time so the meeting ends on time	Doesn't make time for introductions, allows the discussion to go anywhere, with no clear action items, and ends late

A Good Seller ...	A Bad Seller ...
Provides follow-up that recaps the meeting and includes relevant content to prepare for next meeting	Does not follow up the meeting in writing or enter notes into CRM
Customizes his or her materials with the customer's name and relevant imagery (i.e., logo)	Uses the same template for every buyer

EMOTIONS MATTER

A wide range of research shows that most people buy based on emotion, not logic; therefore, it's important to make a deep connection with a prospect by bringing your own vibe into the meeting. That will help people connect with your energy, build momentum, and want to do business with you.

"Energy (vibe) is a supercharger—a force multiplier—for every facet of your life, whether you're an individual who leads yourself and/or your family, you're a leader of a small or large team, or you're the leader of an entire organization."
—Tony Jeary, *Vibe*

When things first started closing down worldwide due to the pandemic, Tony was actually in the air on his way to Australia to speak to a group of over ten thousand people. On his way to the client's office, he was advised that the live event had been cancelled but that they were going to conduct the biggest and best Zoom event ever for this company. They had already hired a giant AV team and acquired all the equipment they needed, and they quickly put together a four-hour virtual event! Tony orchestrated a number of different elements for this event. He asked the executives to take off their ties to help them loosen up and be more relatable to a virtual audience. When the meeting first started, they included the participants in their interactions backstage, which allowed them to feel like they were actually there in person as they experienced the behind-the-scenes dialogue and laughter. Tony also orchestrated the backstage crew to give the event an excitement where everyone was engaged, because no one knew exactly what was coming up next. Most importantly, the president who hired Tony said, "I was worried this would be our worst meeting and it turned out to be one of our best. Part of the reason for this success was because of the incredible vibe that came through the camera!"

Perhaps the most important element of building rapport is trust, which often involves the customers' ability to sense your empathy with their perspective. You can also build trust by being an expert in your offering and being able to articulate its capabilities. One way to do this is to send credible information before your meeting to set the stage for your first conversation. You could also leverage a credible referral as an introduction. Utilize those mutual connections you found in your research.

Creating trust is the most important element of building rapport.

Being dependable and honoring your commitments will build trust as well. Buyers have often been burned in some way before, and integrity matters to them. Be authentic. Be your best "you," instead of what you believe someone wants you to be. Most buyers don't expect perfection, yet they do expect honesty and openness. **Your authenticity will put the buyer at ease.**

Trust is usually built over time. It is important for your prospects to trust you in order to buy from you, so you need to open yourself up to your buyers. They want to feel that you understand them and that they can relate to you. Find ways to spotlight similarities and shared experiences. In your research, discover as much as you can about your buyers' family, where they're from, where they went to school, what their interests are, what companies they've worked for, and what positions they've held. Use opportunities in conversation to share similarities.

Finally, show your commitment to help. When buyers feel you have a genuine interest in helping them, it builds trust. Take the time to learn about them and lay the groundwork for earning their business. This investment will pay major dividends over time.

STEP 2: UNDERSTANDING AND SOLVING YOUR CUSTOMER'S PROBLEMS

The ability to understand the buyer's problem is fundamental to mastery. It's easy to think you know what is most important to a buyer from a first impression or a snippet of a conversation. However, we've seen time and again in the selling realm the power of active listening—both in identifying the actual problem and in helping prospects more clearly articulate what their "ideal state" looks like.

Listening is the key to understanding the buyer's unmet needs. On average, top B2B sales professionals speak 43% of the time and allow the prospect to speak 57% of the time.

Listening is a key piece to understanding a buyer's *unmet needs*. People want to be heard, and that requires listening well. It can be tempting to do too much talking, yet listening is where you will learn the most about your prospects and what they really want and need. Saleshacker.com used AI to analyze 26,537 B2B sales and

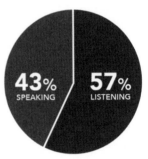

Ratio of speaking to listening in successful B2B sales.

found "top-producing B2B sales professionals speak 43% of the time (on average), allowing the prospect to speak 57% of the time (on average)." The article went on to say that "most sales reps are talking more than they believe they are (65–75% of the call)."[2]

Listening often does not come naturally, especially since many salespeople are extroverts who, by nature, think by talking. It takes extra effort to train yourself to sense when you need to listen.

Everyone loves to talk about themselves. However, what sets masters apart is their ability to let the other person talk as well as their skill in guiding the conversation by asking thoughtful, relevant questions. Great questions can help open up a gold mine of information that can be the difference that closes the deal.

Part of this process is a willingness to get comfortable with even a little bit of silence in order to give others time to think. This takes a conscious effort, and it can be more strenuous than talking. Be willing to practice listening until it becomes a habit.

WHEN MULTIPLE PEOPLE NEED TO SAY YES

You often have multiple stakeholders in a selling situation, and understanding the needs of each stakeholder is important. What is important to one may not matter as much to another, yet if the whole need isn't met, it could affect the outcome of the sale.

Different people also have varying levels of influence in awarding you the business. Make sure you know all the stakeholders in the game and what is important to each so you are not blindsided along the way. This is something that may not always be on the mind of the buyers, so sometimes this discussion can help ensure they are able to sell what they want internally as well.

Be strategic about showing the value of your offering to each stakeholder.

> *There are often multiple stakeholders in a selling situation. Make sure you know who all the stakeholders are and what is important to each.*

Sellers need the most current information—including market conditions, customer insights, competitive intelligence, and even relevant win/loss stories—in order to provide insight and help buyers make decisions. In the past, sales teams often shared these tips from the field in weekly meetings and when salespeople were gathered around the proverbial water cooler. However, post pandemic there are new ways that teams have discovered to share the same type of information, using the power of short videos to share stories, intelligence, and ideas. You will hear more about this in chapter 5.

It isn't enough to understand the current market environment. You have to be able to solve your customer's problems in order to close the deal. There are several strategies for this process. One is to be able to articulate the future state to your clients. Future state considers where the buyers want to go and takes them there. What do they want to create? If they achieved this, how would it affect them and their business?

Then, once you have taken them to where they want to be in the future, share with them why you are the solution for getting there. Show the value you bring and help them see you in that future picture.

Your buyers have gaps, or they wouldn't need you. Right? Part of being a problem solver is showing them why you are the solution and what differentiates you from your competition. Your ability to creatively and clearly present your distinctions by articulating those differences matters. Masters practice how they articulate their value proposition and tailor a selective part of it to each buyer because they understand that you never get a second chance to make a first impression.

> *You never get a second chance to make a first impression. Masters understand this, so they practice how they articulate their value proposition until they get it right.*

To be a problem solver, you need to be able to remove obstacles for the buyer. Before your meeting, create a list of possible objections, along with your solutions. Prepare for the what-ifs in advance. Be prepared for the most likely scenarios. Using a visual to help the buyer understand the process can help set the right expectations. This will allow you to dispel any objections the buyers may have to your offering. Make it easy for the buyer to say yes.

There are a number of sales methodologies that are still applicable to both in-person selling and virtual selling.

Examples include Corporate Visions, SPARXiQ, Solution Selling, SPIN Selling, the ValueSelling Framework, the Sandler Selling System, the Challenger Sales Model, RAIN Group, and hybrids developed internally by many sales organizations. They can be incorporated into your selling strategy, whether they have three steps or ten.

STEP 3. LEVERAGING SUCCESS

Master sellers don't end their engagement after the signature; they protect their reputation by making sure they deliver value to their customers. In fact, the worst thing a seller can do is to move on after the sale is completed. Become a partner to your buyers by ensuring their success, as you promised. Then celebrate their success with them, which will remind them of your value. This will create customers for life, not just one-time customers, which is especially important in B2B sales.

Get feedback on how you can improve. You can always move up to another level of performance, so be open to hearing from your customers how you can be even better. This is an exercise you can do with yourself as well. Ask yourself what you could do in the future to create an even better and more successful experience for your customers.

Follow through on both the sale and the relationship. Let your customers know you're there to stay and that you're flexible when adjustments need to be made. Look for other opportunities to add on products or services that will meet their needs and ask them to refer you to others who will benefit from your offerings.

Most sellers miss the highest value they can derive from a successful sell by stopping short of ensuring buyers provide referrals to additional buyers. Referrals give you an instant advantage with a new buyer, and they give you credibility that often takes months to create. In fact, the "three Rs"—repurchase, referral, and reference—are an essential concept in leveraging success, and all three depend on delivering the value you promised as well as the quality of your ongoing relationship with your buyers.

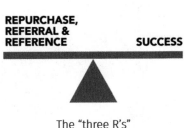

The "three R's"

Delivering the value you promised and maintaining a quality ongoing relationship with your buyers will go a long way toward obtaining the "three Rs"—repurchase, referral, and reference.

At the beginning of this chapter, we discussed two complementary ideas: masters sellers (1) think of modern selling as a *service* to the buyer and (2) fuse the buying cycle and the selling cycle as two sides of the same coin.

"If you cannot tell the difference and thus do not know which piano is right for you, I haven't yet succeeded."
—Erica Feidner

Erica Feidner

This mindset and approach are exemplified by Erica Feidner, known as "The Piano Matchmaker," who is widely considered *one of the greatest salespeople living today.* She was the top sales executive at Steinway & Sons for eight consecutive years. In those eight years, she sold over 41 million dollars' worth of pianos. She was also highlighted in *Inc.* magazine as one of the *top ten salespeople of all time,* along with people like Dale Carnegie and Zig Ziglar.

What are the keys (no pun intended) to Feidner's success? As a master seller, she has two important characteristics: passion and knowledge.

A talented concert pianist herself (she started playing at the age of three), Feidner knows that every pianist is different, and so is every piano. Therefore, every pianist, regardless of skill, has a piano out there that is perfect for him or her; with that mindset, Feidner merely positions herself to help customers find the right instrument.

She treats every case as unique; she listens to each customer play to get an idea of his or her technique, and then she tries the customer out on different pianos until both she and her customer believe they have found the right match. And she is passionate about this. She won't just go for the quick sale; in fact, she refuses to sell a piano she doesn't believe is the right match for her customers. The results speak for themselves: to date, every single one of Feidner's customers has stuck with the piano she has selected for him or her.

Regardless of whether you sell B2B or B2C, there are lessons we can learn from Feidner when it comes to selling. These include having a passion for your chosen profession, understanding that you can't just use the same techniques for every customer, and developing a mindset that allows you to tailor your approach so the customer sees it as a service you're providing.

Feidner epitomizes the master seller—one who ensures his or her buyers are successful so they will buy again and are happy to both provide referrals and serve as a reference (again, the three Rs: repurchase, referral, and reference).

Once you learn to create a harmonious balance between the selling and buying cycles by embracing these key selling imperatives, you will be able to master the art of selling. And the first step in mastering virtual selling is mastering the powerful art of orchestration, which we talk about in chapter 2.

TAKEAWAYS

▶ Mastering virtual selling starts with mastering the art of selling. Those who have worked hard to master face-to-face selling will be able to transition to virtual selling by leveraging their existing skills and learning new ones.

▶ Good selling is grounded in creating an exceptional buying experience. Successful sellers think about selling as a *service* to the buyer, and they fuse the selling cycle with the buying cycle so they are two sides of the same coin.

▶ Creating a harmonious balance between the two cycles involves:

  ▷ researching and building rapport;

  ▷ understanding and solving your buyer's problems; and

  ▷ leveraging success.

▶ Curiosity is one of the most valuable traits a salesperson can have. At a minimum, research your buyer's LinkedIn profile, Google your contact and his or her company, and study the company's website. Master sellers will also look to see whether they can find common connections in their buyers' LinkedIn accounts and contact them to glean what insights they can share about the buyer and the buyer's company.

▶ Creating trust is the most important element of building rapport.

▶ People want to be heard, and that requires listening well. On average, the most successful B2B salespeople talk 43 percent of the time and listen 57 percent of the time.

▶ There are often multiple stakeholders in a selling situation. Make sure you know who all the stakeholders are and what is important to each so you are not blindsided along the way.

▶ You never get a second chance to make a first impression. Masters understand this, so they practice how they articulate their value proposition and tailor a selective part of it to each buyer.

▶ The "three Rs"—repurchase, referral, and reference—are an essential concept in leveraging success, and all three depend on delivering the value you promised as well as the quality of your ongoing relationship with your buyers.

▶ Erica Feidner, known as "The Piano Matchmaker," is widely considered *one of the greatest salespeople living today.* Lessons we can learn from her when it comes to selling are (1) having a passion for your chosen profession, (2) understanding that you can't just use the same techniques for every customer, and (3) developing a mindset that allows you to tailor your approach so the customer sees it as a service you're providing.

ENDNOTES

1 Lori Wizdo, "B2B Buyer Journey Map Basics," Forrester, https://go.forrester.com/blogs/15-05-25-b2b_buyer_journey_map_basics/.

2 Chris Orlob, "Talk Less, Listen More. Do you Know the Golden Talk vs Listening Ratio?" https://www.saleshacker.com/sales-ratio-talk-vs-listening/.

THE POWER OF ORCHESTRATION

chapter 2

"At age 45, after conducting for 20 years, I had a realization. The conductor of an orchestra doesn't make a sound; he depends for his power on his ability to make other people powerful. I realized my job was to awaken possibility in other people."
—Benjamin Zander,
coauthor, *The Art of Possibility*

Ben Zander

Benjamin Zander is a British American conductor who is the founder and music director of the Boston Philharmonic Orchestra and the Boston Philharmonic Youth Orchestra. For the past fifty years, Zander has had a unique role as a master teacher, insightful musical interpreter, and source of inspiration for audiences, students, professional musicians, corporate leaders, politicians, and many others.

Zander's Ted Talk, "The Transformative Power of Classical Music," has been viewed over 20 million times. He is a maestro—a master teacher—who is also *a master of virtual selling*, not only through his TED talk but also through his numerous online classes about music. (His website is www.benjaminzander.com.)

Zander's performances are spellbinding, both because of his delivery and his engagement with the audience, as he brings energy, enthusiasm, and caring to every interaction. He considers those three attributes—especially caring—to be the most crucial to making a difference. Zander's philosophy embodies the mission of this book: teaching you how the greatest sellers master the art of orchestration for success.

Ben Zander's philosophy embodies the mission of this book: teaching you how the greatest sellers master the art of orchestration for success.

A NEW KIND OF MUSIC

Think of selling as a musical event. You, as the conductor, set the stage for an experience, carefully choreograph each performance segment, finely tune them to keep the audience engaged, and bring emotion and rhythm that can be transformative. In both music and virtual selling, there exists a buoyancy, vitality, and energy.

In both music and virtual selling, there exists a buoyancy, vitality, and energy.

LESSONS FROM THE MASTER—OR MAESTRO

Mark had an interesting experience related to Zander's book *The Art of Possibility*. After watching his Ted Talk, Mark decided he would like to see Zander conduct in person. Knowing Mark was a fan, his brother Scott suggested they go to see Zander speak at an event in Boston. But when Mark went online to purchase tickets, he discovered the event was sold out.

Having read Zander's book, which he coauthored with his former wife, psychotherapist Rosamund Zander, Mark did something that, in hindsight, could have been a story from that book. After searching on the Internet, he found a phone number for Zander. He decided to call the number and was expecting to get a voice mailbox or an assistant, but to his surprise, Zander answered the phone. Mark reacted by saying, "Maestro?" to which Zander replied, "Yes!" with a hearty laugh and then, "Who is this?"

Mark told him that he and his brother really wanted to come to his talk, but they were unable to get tickets. He replied that his talk was indeed sold out but that he was doing a separate, private corporate event the following evening, and he invited Mark and his brother to be his guests.

Mark's experience at that event served as an epiphany for him. He first met Zander "backstage," before he was ready to begin his presentation, and he watched as Zander coordinated the people who would assist him in his presentation and concert while simultaneously rehearsing the sequence of how things would go. Then he seamlessly transitioned from the backstage area to the "frontstage," in front of the live audience, where, as always, Zander was able to interact with and delight those in attendance. Then after his talk, he again presented himself "backstage"—off "frontstage" and out of the limelight—as he interacted with the audience informally but continued to engage them and enhance their experience.

Mark was struck with the realization that the totality of this event included activities that had begun long before that evening and did not end with Zander's stepping off the stage. Although the capstone of the experience was the actual live event, in essence, the complete cycle had begun with much preparation beforehand and had ended with continued collaboration with the audience afterward. It was all part of the same experience, but the moving parts had all taken place at different times and in different places, depending on the stage of the event, and they had all been orchestrated to create an exceptional experience for the audience.

Our framework for virtual selling is similarly defined by two arenas: frontstage and backstage. The frontstage of a virtual buying experience is based primarily on synchronous collaboration, where you and the participants have live *virtual* interactions with each other through a Zoom meeting, a phone call, or other means, versus in person. In backstage, you interact with your buyers in an asynchronous way, meaning you may send them an email or something else that they may consume and respond to later, based on their schedule.

Or you may collaborate with a buyer digitally with no requirement for both parties to be locked into a time to do so. Of course, there's much more to the backstage in virtual selling than just sending emails, and we will go into that in depth in chapter 4.

Here is a visual depiction of the process at its highest level. (By the way, the framework we've shared here works for *virtual* as well as *hybrid* selling of the future—a combination of in-person and virtual meetings. When we are able to go back to hybrid selling, you can swap the "virtual" for "in-person" and tweak some of the content shared, and the framework still holds.)

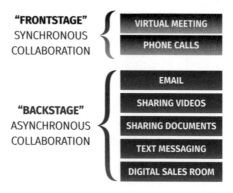

Frontstage and backstage collaborations

THE MAESTRO IS YOU

"Maestro," in Italian, means master teacher. In the context of this book, the maestro—or conductor—is you, the salesperson. A maestro helps the orchestra play to its fullest potential and ensures everything works together to create the desired experience for the audience.

You have the opportunity in virtual selling to create an extraordinary experience for your buyer by orchestrating the frontstage and backstage elements to achieve your desired outcome.

You do the same for your buyers and members of your sales team. By mastering virtual selling, you have the opportunity to create an exceptional buying experience for your buyer by orchestrating the frontstage and backstage activities of a repeatable sales process to achieve sales success.

Ben Zander and Mark Magnacca—backstage

Here's a relevant sidenote: Zander's Ted Talk that Mark watched was filmed in 2008, and yet Mark didn't watch it until 2011—three years after it was initially recorded, which is a testament to the long life and power of the recorded word (in video or print).

DELIVER AN EXCEPTIONAL BUYING EXPERIENCE

In the next two chapters, we will be talking about these two different "stages" from which you will be orchestrating key selling activities to deliver an exceptional buying experience: frontstage and backstage.

You will learn how to orchestrate what happens before, during, and after a frontstage virtual meeting, which we call a backstage "**micro buying experience**," and how you can "**create presence in your absence**" in backstage with your buyers in between meetings.

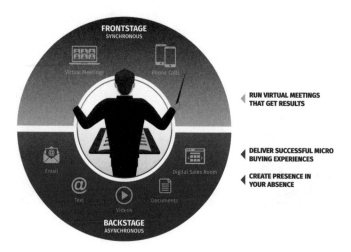

Orchestrate the micro buying experience

Just as you had to learn certain skills to operate successfully in an in-person business meeting—such as how to shake hands correctly and what kind of clothes to wear—you will need to learn a host of new skills that will add value to your buyers from your virtual frontstage to your virtual backstage arena. We will be talking about this in the next two chapters.

Virtual Selling Myths

There are many myths that permeate the collective psyche of salespeople around the world. These myths can hold you back from harnessing the full power of virtual selling. They can also hinder your understanding of how it will continue to be part of the sales process and improve the buyer's experience going forward, even if you are in an industry that does a complete or partial return to office work.

Many people believe that virtual selling is new and only came into being as of March 2020 with the start of the global pandemic. However, virtual selling has actually been around for decades—just in a different form.

Think about how sales have been affected through virtual selling over the past few decades through the telephone, the mail (think print catalogs), electronic media (email and text), and mobile phones. Smart phones, used by billions of people today, have become the modern tool of virtual selling and buying.

In addition to debunking the myth that virtual selling is new, let's examine and debunk five additional myths that are the biggest obstacles to virtual sales success.

MYTH #1: Virtual selling is a *temporary* solution.

According to the American Marketing Association, this change had been coming all along, but the pandemic expedited the speed of the change. As a society, we were already getting an education, working, and "hanging out" with friends online. There are sure to be massive lasting changes to consumer behavior.[1]

While we do not believe that virtual experiences will completely replace our need for face-to-face human interaction, virtual selling is here to stay. COVID proved we can quickly find alternatives to meeting in person. We believe that capitalizing on the benefits of virtual selling is absolutely critical for your future success. As more businesses reopen for travel and incorporate some level of face-to-face engagement, many organizations globally will continue to use virtual selling along with hybrid models of interaction.

People around the world have proven to themselves that virtual meetings are a better way to interact in the buying and selling process for many products and services.

MYTH #2: Virtual selling is inferior to face-to-face selling.

A persistent myth about virtual selling is that it is inferior to face-to-face selling. Even though there may be some factors that are critical in face-to-face selling to get the best results possible, in many ways virtual selling can be better and even more efficient. Virtual selling allows a richer set of participants, both buyers and sellers, since physical place and time (across both the frontstage and backstage areas) are no longer a limitation to collaboration. Additionally, you have a collection of tools in the frontstage and backstage arsenals that help you provide experiences for your buyers that can be far superior to in-person meetings. In this book, we show that virtual selling exposes new dimensions for connecting with clients that were not available before.

Here is a case in point: Two months into the pandemic, a sales call was scheduled with a salesperson we know and an executive at a company located in New York City as well as three members of his team. The virtual meeting began at 1:00 p.m., with everyone present except the executive. At 1:03 the executive texted one of the three junior people who were all on the Zoom call to say he was very sorry but he could not make the meeting, and he asked him to please reschedule the meeting. The remaining group on the call spoke for another five minutes to learn a little more about what the demo should look like during the next call. The prospect said, "I'm sorry we wasted this time, but I don't feel nearly as badly as I would have if you had flown to New York for this meeting." How can most business leaders justify the cost of traveling in person in terms of money, time, and energy for a first appointment with a prospect until the salesperson has had at least a first discovery meeting, virtually? This call was a small example of why virtual is often better than in person, especially for a first meeting. If you cannot get someone to attend a virtual meeting as step one, the odds are low that you will get them to an in-person meeting instead. This is the key takeaway that dispels the myth that virtual selling is inferior to face-to-face selling.

MYTH #3: Virtual selling doesn't require new skills.

Being a good seller does not automatically make you good at virtual selling. Effective virtual selling depends on learning a full range of new skills and knowledge. A master virtual seller will need new skills for running meetings, which are vastly different than an in-person format. They will also need to learn new ways of conveying information and collaborating "backstage" asynchronously, new ways to build rapport and relationships, and much more. Being good at virtual selling requires a commitment to learning new things (which are shared in this book), versus assuming you have all the required skills because you were a good face-to-face seller. We will be talking more about all this in the coming chapters.

MYTH #4: It's hard to build rapport virtually.

On the surface, it's challenging to connect and build trust with people when you can't be with them in person. But we believe this is *only* true at the beginning of the relationship *or* if the seller makes no attempt to modify the way they are engaging with the buyer.

In this book, we share many ways to build rapport effectively in virtual meetings and "create presence in your absence" with buyers through backstage selling activities.

Yes, it is different and therefore more challenging at the beginning. We believe you can turn this into an advantage because other sellers who are competing for the business are experiencing the same issue, and yo̶u̶ advantage mastering this new way of eng̶a̶ buyers. Because of the ease of interacting w̶i̶t̶h̶ ̶b̶u̶y̶e̶r̶s̶ ̶v̶i̶r tually and the increased frequency of engaging the buyer (via both frontstage and backstage), once you are able to break through, you can build very strong relationships over time and create an even stronger bond in the long run.

You can imagine your ability to sell to a buyer looks like the figure below. It starts out slowly in the relationship because it's more challenging initially. But once you've passed a threshold where the buyer believes you are adding value to his/her buying process, your relationship and productivity in the selling/buying cycle will acceler-ate—because virtual selling fundamentally is more effi-cient at communicating and collaborating than before .

Virtual Selling Curve

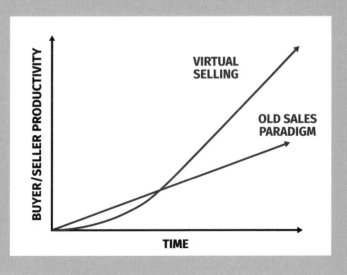

MYTH #5: Buyers are not ready for virtual selling.

According to McKinsey, buyers have grown to enjoy the speed and convenience—not to mention the safety—of remote interactions. Their studies show that "only about 20 percent of B2B buyers say they hope to return to in-person sales, even in sectors where field sales models have traditionally dominated, such as pharma and medical products." And this sentiment has steadily intensified, even after lockdowns have ended.[2]

The truth is, even though many sellers are eager to go back to meeting buyers face-to-face, most buyers are not inclined to meet sellers in person. What they do want is to save time and to efficiently find solutions to their problems, and they want experts to help them make the right decisions. In today's Internet's world, buyers often do their homework online before even deciding who is on their list of vendors to bring into the buying process. For most business-to-business decisions, the pandemic has shown us that face-to-face meetings are not required to conduct business. Even if there are still some buyers who prefer face-to-face contact, the frequency will be less. That means there will be an increasing pressure on you to become a master at virtual selling.

TAKEAWAYS

▶ When you think about yourself as the "maestro" who is orchestrating an exceptional experience for your buyer, it infuses a new sense of purpose or meaning to your interactions in the buying process. Orchestration starts with backstage planning before the "event" happens during the live frontstage meeting and then happens again as "backstage" activities that support a strong finish to the event and continue to create presence in your absence in between.

▶ We have dispelled five myths of virtual selling and demonstrated why this skill set will be critical to your success. Focus on how to utilize every possible resource available to you and maximize them to contribute to your success.

▶ Whether you are a seasoned salesperson or just getting started, rethinking the truths about virtual selling will help you succeed.

▶ We now challenge you to change your perspective moving forward to see how powerful virtual selling can be for your business.

ENDNOTES

1 Mathew Sweezey, AMA, "The Big Shift: A Prediction of What's to Come Post Pandemic," https://www.ama.org/marketing-news/the-big-shift-a-prediction-of-whats-to-come-post-pandemic/.

2 Arnau Bages-Amat, Liz Harrison, Dennis Spillecke, and Jennifer Stanley, "These eight charts show how COVID-19 has changed B2B sales forever," McKinsey & Company, https://www.mckinsey.com/business-functions/marketing-and-sales/our-insights/these-eight-charts-show-how-covid-19-has-changed-b2b-sales-forever#.

FRONTSTAGE
SELLING

chapter 3

"All the world's a stage."
—William Shakespeare

I n the world of virtual selling, the frontstage and
backstage realms are two sides of the same coin. Both
must work seamlessly together to create an exceptional
experience for the customer. And as is the case with a
symphony concert, the backstage activities are what make
the frontstage event possible. In this chapter, we cover the
frontstage area of the virtual selling experience, which is the
live, synchronous, collaborative interaction with the buyer.

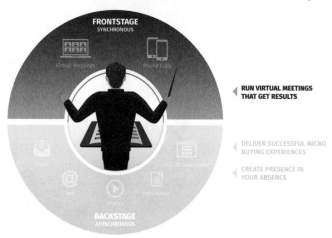

Frontstage selling

FRONTSTAGE CHALLENGES
AND OPPORTUNITIES

In the frontstage arena, you will find both challenges
and opportunities, just as you do with any worthwhile

endeavor. Generally speaking, here are some of the challenges you will face:

▶ Building rapport. In virtual selling, it is harder initially to establish human-to-human connections than with in-person meetings.

▶ Reading people. It's harder to read people through a headshot on a monitor, which makes it more difficult to pick up on nuances such as body language. You can see facial expressions and pick up on tonality, of course, but they're still flat, so you can't read them in a three-dimensional way.

▶ Keeping people's attention. You're often blind to what people are doing at the moment. Since the camera allows only limited visibility, people may be more tempted to multitask. If you don't know how to keep their attention, they could be sending a text or reading something beyond the camera's eye. And since you don't control the environment, anything could happen. A family member could walk by—maybe a child or even an animal—and cause a major distraction or even a disruption.

Fortunately, the opportunities in the frontstage arena often outweigh the challenges when you master this new way of selling.

▶ Time efficiency. Because there is no travel or commute time involved, you can do five to ten times more virtual meetings, once you become proficient at them, than you can in-person meetings.

▶ Effectiveness. You can leverage many more components that are unique to virtual selling, such as all the elements of a frontstage arsenal (which we will discuss later in this chapter).

▶ Opportunity. As we said in the introduction, everyone is an apprentice. You're all now on a level playing field that is different, even somewhat difficult, for everyone—including your competitors—so it's easier to get ahead, even without experience!

KEY ELEMENTS FOR TACKLING FRONTSTAGE SELLING

1. Make Every Minute Count

In order to keep your audience's attention, one of the most important elements of executing frontstage selling is *making every minute count*. Here are several ways you can optimize your frontstage time:

Keep your audience's attention in frontstage selling by making every minute count!

Agenda. Rethink your agenda. Make sure you only do the things in frontstage that you can't do backstage. For example, invest your

frontstage time in collaboration (back and
forth) with your buyer and move your one-way
presentations to backstage. If you must make a
presentation frontstage, tailor your messaging
in a digital format that keeps your audience
engaged and use the **"one-third rule"**. If you
normally give a sixty-minute presentation,
cut it down to perhaps twenty minutes. If you
typically include less than thirty words on a
slide, reduce that to *ten* words per slide. To help
you make the transition, we have a tool on how
to design new agendas later in this chapter, in
the frontstage arsenal section.

Fluency. Become fluent at running a virtual
meeting. Keep the meeting short and make it
interesting. In an in-person meeting, you may get
people to stay with you even if you ramble for a
bit. Not so with a virtual meeting. Wasting even a
few minutes is a huge deal.

*Keep your virtual meeting short
and make it interesting. Wasting
even a few minutes in a virtual
meeting is a huge deal!*

It's crucial that you use a repeatable template
(see samples in the frontstage arsenal) so you can
be fluent at these meetings. Mastery is based on
repetition. To help with fluency, you can actually
keep bulleted notes right next to the camera to

remind you of key things to cover without your audience even knowing it. This is something you can't do in in-person meetings. But in your quest to strive for fluency, be sure you don't come across as reading from notes!

Meeting Increments. Schedule meetings at twenty-five- or fifty-five-minute increments (versus thirty- or sixty-minute meetings) so you have a transition time to prepare and be efficient for your next call. Just because you can schedule virtual meetings one after another doesn't mean you should! Slotting time in between meetings gives you time to catch your breath, reset your mind, take a bathroom break, prepare for the next meeting, or even text someone or make a short call if you need to. Without that extra time, there's no way you can be at peak performance and be fully present for your next meeting.

2. **Find New Ways to Build Trust and Rapport**
   Building trust and rapport is critical in sales success; however, you must fine-tune and build muscle on a few key aspects of your people skills for virtual selling. Here are some ideas that work:

   Use Virtual Meetings. Use virtual meetings so you can see your buyers—versus a phone call—as much as possible. It's much easier to connect with someone when you can see each other's faces, versus just hearing a voice.

So, just like your signature is unique, think about the unique ways you can connect with buyers to make a difference. (In the frontstage arsenal, you will find a larger list of sample content that helps build trust and rapport.)

Build in Getting-to-Know-You Time. Leave five or ten minutes either at the beginning or at the end of your call to chat about anything other than your agenda items so there is an opportunity to make a connection and build rapport. Note this is different from the buffer time *between* meetings mentioned earlier. This is about having room in the agenda for some personal rapport building.

Find Commonality. Look for appropriate ways to find commonality in the background components you see behind the person(s) you're meeting with. For example, you could ask about their artwork, or you could say, "Is that a keyboard I see behind you? Do you play? Music is something I'm passionate about as well." Be sure you don't come across like you're a member of the FBI by being too intrusive. Think of this approach as an interview on a talk show versus an interrogation. By being authentic, you can set the stage for fostering rapport.

Customize Your Own Background. By all means, be sure your viewable background is clean and neat. If you can, include components that tell an interesting story about you or your company that may prompt rapport-building questions from your buyer. Think about your own background as part of how you "set the stage." As an example, leaving a closet door open in view of the camera is both a distraction and does not send the right message. The right background can help build a connection and rapport. If your actual setting does not facilitate the right message, most of the leading **virtual meeting platforms** allow for you to use a virtual background that can also be a great way to make a connection with your buyer. Using a custom virtual background can also help you to build your own personal brand. This can be a consistent reminder about you, both frontstage and when you are doing "backstage" follow-up when using a short recap video.

In addition, pay close attention to your attire. Be aware that the way you dress carries a message. For example, it may be more appropriate to wear a jacket vs. just a dress shirt, depending on your industry. Or it may be appropriate for you (and your team if there are others on the call) to wear branded clothing. Prior to COVID, before we were all working heavily through flat screens, the people who wore branded clothes for work were mostly professional athletes. Now, that seems to be part of the game for everyone. And here's an observation: wear solid or near-solid colors if you can, as prints can often be a distraction.

Be aware that the way you dress in a virtual meeting carries a message.

Send Food, Drinks, or "Meeting Kits."
Nothing builds rapport better than breaking bread together. Right? You can instill the fun factor and rack up "brownie points" (pun intended) by sending ahead food, drink, and "**meeting kits**" to your buyers and their teams. If you have five people together on a Zoom call and you're all eating the same cupcakes, it's a great shared experience and rapport-building opportunity. With all the delivery options out there today, this has never been easier to do, even if your buyers are in different cities.

For more important meetings, send "meeting kits," which are custom-built packages that contain tailored items you will be referring to during the meetings.

You can create a great shared experience and rapport-building opportunity by sending food ahead of time and "breaking bread" together while you're on the Zoom call.

Because of the cost and effort involved in creating meeting kits, this activity should be reserved for the most important meetings and should ideally be repeatable with other buyers. With respect to the cost and effort, remember, this is still simpler and cheaper than flying to see clients as you did in the pre-pandemic days! Once you get the routine down, repeating the same meeting kit for different clients will be easier. Ask your company for additional help once this is working for you and others. Here are some examples of meeting kits and their content:

In this kit, the theme of the virtual meeting was "courage." The meeting host wanted to use different items related to the theme that participants could open at different times of the meeting.

The theme of this meeting was "brainstorming." Participants were directed to open different items throughout the meeting, which helped create a shared experience. (Meeting kit resources and links are available at *masteringvirtualselling.com*)

Use Discovery Questions. If your buyer is talking, they are automatically engaged. Facilitate by using effective discovery questions (again without interrogating), so you can build rapport quickly. One of Tony's favorite statements is the invitation to "tell me more." This phrase is a big winner that makes people feel you're into them, their thinking, and their message—and you are.

Use Appropriate Humor. Humor creates an atmosphere of fun, dissolves tension, keeps the meeting interesting, and builds rapport. Tony gives out one-dollar bills to people in his in-person audiences, and he has a plaque he shows his virtual audiences that has a dollar bill on it and says people get a dollar for "brilliance, humor, and compliments." When he shows the plaque on camera, participants are wowed, or at least intrigued. When he gives out "digital dollars," he always gets a laugh or at least a smile. That type of atmosphere helps break up a monotonous meeting and encourages engagement. Note: If you're not naturally funny, and most people aren't, then perhaps you can read things that are funny or show a funny video clip that is relevant to the discussion. But keep testing and stay authentic until you find things that work for you.

Understand *You* Can Make a Difference. There are some who believe we are moving into a world where the salesperson will not matter and a machine using AI will replace the human element, but the post-pandemic world has shown that people still want to buy from people. The best virtual sellers have mastered the ability to bring their authentic selves to the buying journey. Your ability to connect with people in the virtual realm, with your own authentic style, is as critical as it is with in-person selling. In the first chapter, we discussed how Erica Feidner did this by sharing her passion for the piano and helping her buyers get

to know her, which only added to h
as a seller. You can do this in multip
example, Tony is well known to his
use of props, which include books, coins, flags, and
other cool visuals he uses to reinforce a point in a
virtual meeting. Mark regularly uses short videos
that are relevant to the situation to make a point
or shift the dynamic when the situation requires it.
For example, he has been known to share a video
clip from the old *Candid Camera* television program
that causes audiences to laugh and understand a
larger point being made. Yuchun is a master at
creating an image or diagram that captures the
totality of the subject at hand. As an example, his
visuals help Allego customers see the big picture
and understand what it means.

Know How to Read Body Language and Virtual Room Dynamics

When you're in a virtual meeting, be very careful to
observe body language so you will know when the participants are showing interest or disinterest. Check for
signs that show interest, such as:

▶ good eye contact;
▶ active listening skills:
  ▷ leaning in when you're talking;
  ▷ nodding their heads;

▷ positive, enthusiastic facial expressions, such as a genuine smile (versus a fake one); and

▷ active hand gestures.

Check for signs that convey distancing, including:

▶ leaning back;

▶ crossing their arms;

▶ scowling;

▶ slumping/slouching;

▶ looking bored;

▶ multitasking (e.g., checking their phone); and

▶ fiddling.

As far as room dynamics go, they're not that different in virtual meetings than they are in in-person meetings. Train yourself to pay attention to such dynamics as:

▶ tone of voice;

▶ energy level;

▶ level of participation;

▶ evidence of activity (or lack of) during silence (i.e., are they working or just not speaking?);

▶ who speaks first in a group (Morgan Wolan with Red Velvet Events says, "Pay attention to who speaks first. Are they introducing the team, are they an influential supportive role, are they the key decision maker, or are they simply the most extroverted of the bunch? You should seek to engage all players strategically, but know whom to and how to address certain questions."[1])

3. Know What Content Works in Virtual Selling

Some of the content you shared in in-person meetings will be irrelevant and other content will be less effective in a virtual setting.

In today's new world, all of your content should still be grounded in adding value to the buying process, but it must be different in order to be effective. Here are some types of content we found that work better:

Collaboration. The most effective frontstage content often aids in facilitating collaboration (e.g., action plans). The ultimate goal is active engagement in the meeting while flushing out key steps to further the selling/buying process.

One way to facilitate engagement is to show a video and set it up by asking people to write down, say, four things they notice in the video about whatever your subject is; then after the video plays, collaborate with your people on those four elements.

Here's another example of how to facilitate collaboration, and this one involves us. In our coaching sessions with Tony, he developed a situation template for our discussion on HR issues.

As a management team, we collaboratively completed the template in regard to:

▶ Our situation: We have salespeople who fit into three categories—some are A players, some are B players, and some are C players. We can no longer carry C players. We have to move them up to B, either with tools or with training, or move them out.

▶ Our need: We need to create a plan for speeding learning for our C-level players so we can bring them up to a B level in a short amount of time.

▶ Our deliverables. This is the *mutual action plan*, where we assign actions for specific individuals to take over the next ninety days that will bring about the deliverables we are striving to achieve—in this case improving our lagging performers. The beauty of the mutual action plan is that you agree on the actions and who is responsible for them before you log off the call, and it is on the screen for all to see.

This type of content is very engaging. And you get a multilayer win because you're providing great content while you're really connecting as you collaborate together. You can use a template for your action plan with columns and boxes that can be filled in with your content. (You will find a sample in the frontstage arsenal.)

Client:

Attendees:			
Name	Position	Email	Phone

Preparation:
-

Objectives:
-

Agenda:

Strategic Acceleration Language:

1. *HLAs* - Activities that will return the highest impact
2. *Strategic Clarity* - clear understanding (at all levels) based on a clear vision, objectives & strategic plan
3. *Elegant Solution* - an activity that accomplishes multiple objectives/goals
4. *PBP* - Production Before Perfection is thinking, which ensures results start happening vs. being slowed or stuck because of perfectionism
5. *Belief Window* - a model, that describes how one makes choices/decisions/actions based on principles/rules on ones filter
6. *Blind Spots* – things one misses and can't even see in terms of how things are; how they work; or what's even available
7. *Strategic Cascading* - the well-considered, consistent filtering down of messaging throughout an organization
8. *Strategic IQ* - intentional balance between one's strategic & tactical activities

Notes:
-

VIPs/ Force Multipliers:
-

Extras:
1.

Action Next Steps:	Who
1.	
2.	
3.	

Closing Comments/Takeaways:

Situation Template-Tonyjeary.com

Multimedia. It's much easier to bring in multimedia content in a virtual meeting than it is when you're live, in person. In a virtual meeting, everyone is already set up for multimedia and you can play whatever content you want right on the screen. Most people think if they have a PowerPoint deck, they're all set, but there are so many other things you can bring in to be creative. For example, you can use prerecorded videos (which, by the way, provide great "**breathing spaces**" for you) made by the CEO, other executives, or **SMEs** (subject-matter-experts), as well as videos of customer testimonials. Here is an example of a customer, John, providing a testimonial during a meeting, which was later repurposed as a video to allow other prospects and customers to hear about this experience directly from him.

Example customer story captured on
video that could be repurposed

You can also prerecord a condensed version of your presentation to use frontstage (or backstage). A prerecorded presentation can be better and more concise because you can edit and improve it beforehand. Remember to make it one-third as long as you would if you were presenting in person.

The key element with using multimedia is to make sure you prepare for it. If you're going to show people three or four videos, make sure you have them ready, so when you share your screen, you're prepared to play them versus having to fumble around to look for them. Be sure to have them downloaded so you don't have to worry about the video malfunctioning for whatever reason. Even in perfect conditions, playing a video in a virtual meeting directly from the web takes up twice as much bandwidth when compared to playing a predownloaded video! So have the downloads on hand to help avoid the problem of choppy videos.

Support. Get additional support for important calls. It's much easier to get SMEs and other executives involved in the frontstage of a virtual meeting than having to fly them in for in-person meetings. Be the first seller to take advantage of this untapped potential in your company! Even if your CEO can't make it, see if there is a prerecorded video of him or her that you can use on the call. This is actually a huge advantage of virtual selling, and we are convinced it will be widely utilized once everyone starts to realize this. For additional support, you can leverage a manager, peers, or assistants (especially to manage tech for important meetings).

*A huge advantage of virtual selling
is the ability to take advantage of
having executives or SMEs participate
in the meeting, either live on camera
or in a prerecorded video, since you
don't have to fly them in as you would
have to do for in-person meetings.*

Finally, we should emphasize again that, even
though you have more types of content to work
with than before, the key is to be sure to utilize
the ideas in our frontstage arsenal that add value
to your buyers, that are appropriate for the stage
they are in, and that reinforce the selling/buying
process.

4. **Make Effective Use of Technologies and Tools**
    Essential frontstage technologies and tools are:
    lighting, camera, microphone, speakers, Internet
    connections, and, most importantly, your virtual
    meeting tool. In virtual selling, you are totally
    dependent on technology, so you want to make
    sure you use it to its fullest extent.

    **Use a direct-wired connection versus
    wireless.** One of the most basic suggestions we
    have for sellers conducting frontstage selling is to
    use a directly wired Internet connection whenever
    possible! It is a bit more work setting this up,
    but it will save you headaches because you never

know when a Wi-Fi connection will cause you problems. Yes, a wired connection can cause you problems too, but it will be much more reliable than wireless. Don't leave things like this to chance.

Get the Best Tech! Using dated or mediocre technology is like wearing a cheap suit to a meeting.

Be an Expert on Your Tools. Virtual meeting tools anchor frontstage selling, and sellers must be fluent at using these tools. Every seller should have basic knowledge about the common features and know how to select the best sources for each, such as your microphone, speaker, screen sharing, whiteboarding, and chat features. (And you should verify during your frontstage "checklist review" before every call that these features are working properly.) You want to be fluent with all features that are relevant so you can create good habits that will help produce a better meeting experience. For example, turning on the touch-up in Zoom can help provide a better first impression, even if your lighting is not optimal.

You want to be fluent with all features of your virtual meeting tool, including how to select the best sources for each, such as your microphone, speaker, screen sharing, whiteboarding, and chat features.

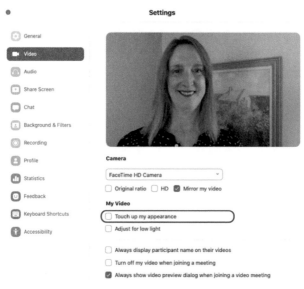

Zoom example of touch-up

In addition, we find it a best practice at the start of a meeting to paste the meeting agenda (in text) in the chat window so all can refer to it throughout the meeting. Another example is to know tips for building good habits when muting your voice. We would all be rich if we had a dollar for every time a person was muted while he/she was talking, or even worse, when people forget to mute their mic while not speaking to the group! Make sure this doesn't happen to you, the person running the meeting. Depending on how often you are to speak, there are shortcuts you can take to make sure you are properly muted most of the time (e.g., on Zoom, a tap on the space bar will mute/unmute you).

Similarly, for screen sharing, it's good to know how your entire screen desktop looks to the audience if you have to share the entire screen. It's a good habit to clean your desktop when you are preparing for a meeting and remove any content, tasks, or interruptions that are unrelated to the meeting. Be sure to have all needed content, open and ready to share with your buyer. Once you get to a higher level of fluency, you can also explore the "Screen Share Only" mode as one application on your desktop. However, this requires that you understand not just the video conference tool, but also the application you are sharing (e.g., Microsoft PowerPoint has numerous presentation modes that require additional knowledge for correct usage). At the end of the day, fluency and habits come from repeating a set routine. Practice makes perfect.

Be Fluent in Other Meeting Technology. It's also a good idea to know virtual meeting tools other than your own since you may be invited to someone else's meeting that uses a different tool. Being fluent gives you a competitive advantage as a master because you can speak everyone's language.

As of the time of this book's publishing, the top five tools being used are:

▶ Zoom

▶ WebEx

▶ Google Meet

▶ Microsoft Teams

▶ GoToMeeting

You can find updates of this list and more details on our supporting website for the book at *www.masteringvirtualselling.com.*

Leverage meeting recordings. A key feature of modern video conferencing tools is their ability to actually record the full call. This is an important feature to leverage because it is, in essence, an automated notetaker and allows a seller to fully concentrate on the meeting, versus jotting down notes while trying to concentrate on listening. Most tools also come with a decent capability to automatically transcribe a call, which allows the entire call to be searchable; this also makes it valuable for follow-up, AI-based analysis, and other value-added activities in the backstage-selling part of the virtual-selling process that we will get into in chapter 4.

You need to ask the participants' permission for the call to be recorded, and this can be automatically done with most virtual meeting tools by default. (It will announce to all participants that the meeting is being recorded when they join the meeting.) Our data shows that people are saying yes much more often to having the meetings recorded than just a year ago. We have found it works best to offer this as a value added for the buyers, explaining that you will share the transcript of the call with them so they won't have to take notes either.

We strongly believe this will be standard practice in the future. Companies that are concerned about "putting things in writing" need to know that it is best to assume all their communications are potentially recorded already. Thinking otherwise will only get a company into trouble in the long run and at the most unexpected time. Recording a call is not much different than what is already happening every day when a seller is sending email, text messaging, calling, or doing virtual meetings. In fact, you can actually reduce risk with your ability to access and leverage AI from time to time to ensure sellers are not saying things that may put the business at risk.

As technology continues to change, of course, more features and shortcuts will emerge. As a master of virtual selling, it's important to keep up with the technology. For example, there are tools now that allow AI analysis of a seller's calls to automatically point out potential "next-best content" to share and areas the seller can improve on, which also enables more effective coaching of new hires. (We call this "game-tape coaching.")

Another new bleeding-edge feature just coming out is email generated by AI that automatically summarizes the meeting, listing, say, the four things you discussed in your forty-five-minute call that you need to do as next steps. These types of technology will get better and better over time. Once they are efficient enough, they will be incredibly useful tools that will save you time and make the buyer's experience and connection to you stronger than your competition's. We will continue to keep tabs on them and update our readers through our supporting website at *www.masteringvirtualselling.com*.

Have a Backup Strategy. Write down (or have quick access to) the conference call-in number! In case of technical difficulties that forestall your virtual meeting, have a strategy in place to switch to a phone call as plan B. For example, having a landline phone connection can be invaluable and is a low-cost alternative that will ensure your ability to immediately pivot to the dial-in number if your Internet connection is lost. Have a hard copy of critical presentation material at hand, in case your computer crashes. These little "insurance policies" should be part of the frontstage checklist and will save you from time to time.

Be sure to have in place a strategy to switch to a phone call as plan B in case of technical difficulties that could forestall your virtual meeting.

As a case in point, in May 2020, Mark was doing a virtual presentation for over 500 people for an Allego client at a financial services firm in Canada. The presentation was based on the key ideas from this book. It was Mark's first experience with the new meeting platform the client had selected. He had been through a rehearsal the week before, and everything had worked perfectly with the screen and the sound. Michelle, the meeting manager, had suggested that he have the dial-in numbers printed out in case there was a technical problem. On the day of the presentation, Mark showed up fifteen minutes early, as requested. From the moment he logged into the meeting, he knew there was a problem. First, Mark could hear the presenter on stage, but Michelle could not hear Mark's audio at all. Mark sent a chat saying, "Call my cell at this number." When Michelle called, he could tell she was quite stressed. She said, "We only have ten minutes before you go live, and we don't know what is happening. The audio feed for the live presentation is not working, even though it worked at rehearsal this morning." That was when Mark realized one item that was *not* on his checklist was his cell phone reception. From his basement home office, it only showed one bar, and Michelle's voice was cutting out. The day before there had been two bars on his cell phone's reception icon, and it was working correctly. Mark started to feel his heart pound as he realized he had just two minutes before he took the stage, and there was a good chance the audience would not hear anything he was saying. That was ironic, as he was speaking as an expert on the topic of virtual selling and communication. At that moment, he remembered that he actually had a landline telephone in his closet. It was not lost on him that the technology from a previous generation worked correctly over 99 percent of the time, and it took less than ten seconds to install and hear that wonderful sound, the dial tone. With sixty seconds to spare, Mark texted Michelle and said he would pivot to the audio-only dial-in number. Michelle said that would work, and that she could push the slides for him that she had from his rehearsal. Mark dialed in and heard his introduction from the MC as it was broadcast to the audience. He began the presentation and simply asked Michelle to click to the next slide as he went through his presentation without missing a beat. As he said goodbye and hung up the phone, he realized the backup strategy had saved the day. Make sure you have one!

Suggestions to Help You Avoid the Most Common Problems:

▶ Poor sound quality: Make sure you have good quality sound, both mic and speakers, for your presentation so it's not distracting for buyers. Ask a peer to sound-check your equipment from a mock meeting when doing a new setup.

▶ Cluttered (computer) desktop: Avoid having files or tabs open that have nothing to do with your presentation.

▶ Forgetting to turn off shared screen mode: Don't leave your shared screen on when you aren't using slides or video so participants can see each other.

▶ Use muting shortcut: Tapping the spacebar allows you to quickly unmute while staying on mute. Build up a strong habit of managing mute!

▶ Hard-to-read meeting material: Participants need to be able to easily read what's on the screen. Learn to do a presentation in full-screen slide mode as a habit, and know how to quickly zoom a document or a web page when sharing your screen (i.e., Control + and Control –).

5. Understand That Perception Is Reality

Know how you are perceived on stage. As a frontstage performer, you must be constantly aware that people are observing you. It's critical that you understand how you are perceived on stage so you can improve and create the perception of a master virtual seller.

In order to do that:

Review Past Videos of Yourself. It's easier now than ever before to review past recordings of your meetings to see how you look. You can also ask other people to review your videos and give you feedback. Have people give you a debriefing afterward, even if it's just by email.

Be Aware Before the Call.

▶ Check your outfit, your background, and the noise level around you.

▶ Check to see where your eyes will be looking when you look at the content on your screen.

Be Aware During the Call.

▶ Pay close attention to your camera status so you will know at all times whether it is turned on or off.

▶ Background noises:

  ▷ Typing. (Recording the call is better than taking notes by typing, unless you have someone else taking live notes who is not close to a mic.)

  ▷ Eating is not appropriate on most calls, unless agreed upon for a joint lunch meeting, etc.

  ▷ Children, dogs, lawn mower, etc. Be sure to manage these as much as possible and mute when they happen anyway.

▶ Be constantly aware of your body language, including putting on a slight smile. Most people, as they age, will have a natural frown. Counter that with a slight tightening of muscles at the edge of your mouth.

▶ Exaggerate your own body language. Typical in-person reactions, such as a head nod, are hard to see in a virtual meeting. Instead, learn to exaggerate your own body language to provide effective feedback, especially the positive ones. For example, an "OK" or a "thumbs up" sign goes a long way toward conveying your approval and can subconsciously nudge your audience to want more of it. (See a good example below that Tony commonly uses.)

Tony Jeary signaling with the "OK" sign that he likes the idea

6. Manage Time and Energy

Keep a Good Command of the Time. You must remain keenly aware of the time during the meeting and find ways to keep the others on the sales call aware of it as well. It's a good idea to review the time element at the beginning of the meeting (as suggested earlier, have the agenda posted in a chat shared with everyone) so any needed adjustments can be made up front. Once you get buy-in from everyone on the time, you've basically confirmed that the decision maker won't be leaving early.

In Tony's book *We've Got to Start Meeting and Emailing Like This*, he says, "One of the best approaches we've found for improving meeting management across an organization is setting—*and following*—written standards for the meeting." These are the standards he recommends, which can easily be adapted to virtual meetings:

1. Have a clear purpose and defined objective(s) for every meeting.

2. Ensure that the right people are either in the room, on the phone, or represented.

3. Create *and follow* a realistic, timed agenda.

4. Start and end meetings on time.

5. Acknowledge that achieving winning outcomes is not just the meeting leader's responsibility but everyone's responsibility.

6. Facilitate for results so everyone stays involved and engaged.

7. Take thorough notes, documenting important discussion points, outcomes, and agreements.

8. Develop a "who-does-what-by-when" action plan.

9. Publish meeting notes and actions plans quickly, and follow up to ensure timely execution.

10. Strategically cascade meeting outcomes promptly and consistently to others in the organization.

Set and communicate ground rules at the start of every meeting. Below are some ground rules you may want to adopt:

▶ Everyone participates.

▶ Take breaks as needed.

▶ Be smart in managing cellular phones, laptops, and tablets.

▶ Post interesting but off-agenda topics for discussion at the end of the session if time permits.

A great *New York Times* article entitled "How to Run a More Effective Meeting" confirms this content, which you can access on our website: *www.masteringvirtualselling.com*.

Consider Offloading Content. It's important to facilitate the meeting in such a way that you don't lose track of time. By briefing everyone several times during the meeting on the amount of time left, you keep a good command of the time and can make decisions about what agenda items to cover in the time remaining. You may have to skip an item or two and offload them to backstage, perhaps addressing the issue later with a video.

Brief everyone on the amount of time left several times during the meeting so you keep a good command of the time remaining and can make decisions about what agenda items to cover in that time.

Manage Energy as Well as Time. That may involve watching the time of day you book the meeting to ensure it's held at a common high-energy time. Or when you see the energy level dropping in a meeting, you may want to make the decision to punt the rest of the agenda to a new time. You might say, "I'm noticing the energy level is a little low right now. I know we have people from around the world in this meeting. Why don't we address the next two steps now and then move the third to tomorrow."

That's facilitating based on energy—reading people and making decisions to your best advantage so you get the buy-in and the action you want. The master constantly studies what they have to work with, in regard to both time and energy.

For Long Meetings, Schedule Breaks. Be sure to schedule time for hydrating, eating a snack, and going to the bathroom if the meeting is longer than one-and-a-half hours. Otherwise, you will lose people during the call. Make sure you have your own water/drinks and snacks handy so you won't have to go find them during the break.

Use an Agreed-upon (Interactive) Agenda. If possible, create the agenda collaboratively with your buyer or a key sponsor, during a short prep call beforehand, to ensure you cover the buyer's needs as well as your own and to avoid any surprises. Put the buyer's needs front and center, and balance rapport building with the buyer's interest.

Use the Roll Call Productively. Be cognizant of the fact that everyone may not show up on time, so you may want to use the first few minutes to build rapport. There may be people on the call from different divisions, and they may not all know each other. So one way to save time and start building rapport right up front is to take screenshots of the top part of each of their LinkedIn accounts and send them out with the meeting invitations. Then during roll call, show the LinkedIn screenshots as you're making the introductions. It helps you facilitate the

introductions faster, as everyone is already
of each person's name, title, and backgrou

Sample screenshots from LinkedIn profiles

Here's a sample script you can use when you send
out these screenshots via email:

"Below please find a screenshot of the LinkedIn
profiles of our confirmed participants to
familiarize you with those in attendance and save
the time of doing introductions."

**Use "Targeted Polling" as a Means to Keep
People's Attention.** It's a good idea to call
people by name as you poll them or ask questions
during the meeting. You will need a list of all
the meeting participants' names, so you can write
them down during roll call, or you can add the
following script to your email invitation:

"When you log into the Zoom call, please rename
yourself with the following format: First and last

name, title, and company. NOTE: To do this, click on your picture and then select 'rename.'"

Follow the "One-Third Rule" Throughout the Meeting. Whatever you would do in an in-person meeting, do only one-third of it during a virtual sales meeting.

Be Aware of the Amount of Time You Are Speaking in Proportion with Others. Remember, you're facilitating the meeting, not making a one-person presentation. As we have said throughout, talk less and listen more. Ask questions and get your buyers engaged so you can fully discover their needs. Top virtual sellers speak less than 43 percent of the time, depending on the number of people on the call.

Another great resource for creating virtual meetings is an article by Selling Power entitled, "How to Lead Your Sales Force to Peak Performance with Zoom (or Any Online Meeting Platform)." We've included a link to this article on our website, *www.masteringvirtualselling.com*.

THERE'S SOMETHING ABOUT MARY . . .

Mary heard the notification chime for her 1:00 p.m. meeting at 12:55 p.m. She realized it was time to do a quick review of her frontstage checklist before her virtual meeting with a large financial services company. The purpose of this meeting was to discuss a content creation and sharing framework with Frank, her business sponsor, and John, the company's chief compliance officer. Mary knew from her brief prep call with Frank that it was important to be succinct and *get to the point fast* with John. She had prepared the agenda and sent it out in advance, and she had planned to show only three slides and an approved customer video. She selected an appropriate background that blurred the brick wall in her home office to minimize any distractions. Mary joined the virtual meeting at 12:57 p.m., and John was already waiting on the call. While they waited for Frank to join, she used the opportunity to build person-to-person rapport by asking a few questions about his prior experience that she had seen on LinkedIn. During their conversation, she learned that she had gone to the same college as John's daughter. At 1:01 p.m., Frank joined the call and said, "It looks like there is no need for introductions, as you two seem to have already met." Mary then pivoted and asked John if he had seen the agenda for the call. He said, "I did see it in your email, but I don't have it in front of me." Without missing a beat, Mary pasted the agenda and said, "Take a look in the chat window and let me know if there is anything you want to add to this agenda." John said it looked good as it was. She then said she would like to record the call to simplify note-taking for everyone and would be glad to share the recording with John after the call. John and Frank both gave their approval. The call followed the plan that Mary and Frank had outlined, and most of the time was invested in back-and-forth dialogue, questions/answers, and brainstorming. In the process, Mary jotted down a list of content items that she would share as follow-up items. At one point, Frank sent a chat privately to Mary saying, "Share the customer example and tell him how this relates to the question he just asked."

Mary had already downloaded the video beforehand, and it was ready to go. As she played the video, she carefully observed John's reaction. She was literally orchestrating the experience for John by managing the slides to set the stage, playing a customer video, gauging John's reactions, listening to his questions, and responding to chats from Frank. At 1:57 she said, "We have three minutes left until the call ends," and she asked John, "What would be most valuable to you as the next step?" John said, "I'd like a copy of your slides and the recording of this call. I want to review with my team, and then let's reconvene in the next two weeks to start drafting our review process." After the call, Mary started her follow-up with John and Frank by creating a personalized video with the slides embedded in it for downloading. In the video, she also thanked the two men for the call, summarized the key points and next steps discussed, and asked John to calendar the next meeting. As she took a pause before the next meeting in twelve minutes, Mary was very pleased with the progress she had made with this account. She was glad she had allowed for thirty minutes between her calls, which had enabled her to switch context and be ready for peak performance again for the next client who needed her expertise in making the right decisions in solving high-impact business problems.

TAKEAWAYS

▶ As you're learning to master the frontstage of your virtual selling experience, it's important that you learn how to make every minute count.

▶ It's crucial that you find new ways to build trust and rapport, as you're running a tighter ship than you did in face-to-face meetings. Leverage new ways to do so in frontstage selling.

▶ Simply being *yourself* is the key to authenticity. The best virtual sellers have mastered the ability to bring their authentic selves to the buying journey.

▶ Learn to read virtual body language and virtual room dynamics to gain insights on your own effectiveness and buyers' interest.

▶ You will need to use new and sometimes very different content in virtual selling than you did in in-person selling, focusing more on interactive collaboration, soliciting support from executives and SMEs, and utilizing multimedia content.

▶ You want to demonstrate when you are in the frontstage area that you are a master virtual seller. Review past videos of yourself, ask your peers for feedback, and be aware before and during the call of such things as your image, your body language, your background, and the noises around you.

▶ Learn to manage energy and time effectively throughout the meeting, create opportunities for buyers to speak, and sprinkle in humor and your own authentic "secret sauce" to keep people engaged and away from multitasking.

▶ Use the best technologies and tools you can find! Then learn all you can about your own virtual meeting tool so you can be the expert, and learn at least the basics about other meeting technologies and features as well.

▶ Always make sure you have a backup plan in case of technology failure!

Now that we've given you the knowledge that will enable you to be a maestro and shown you how to orchestrate the frontstage of virtual selling, we're going to show you in the next chapter how to master the backstage area as well.

Frontstage Arsenal

Content That Works

Below is a list of content we have seen success with when incorporated into frontstage selling. Just as certain elements are used for an in-person meeting, such as how to correctly shake hands, we focus here on content that differs from that used in traditional in-person meetings to highlight what works better in the virtual-selling world:

Virtual Meeting Template. We suggest you start to think about virtual meetings using this premeeting tool at the beginning. The key here is to plan a meeting within a framework that has been proven to get results. Apply this framework to different types of meetings you may have (e.g., introductory, discovery, problem-solving, solution-presentation, solution-recommendation, technical deep-dive, contract-discussion). Over time, you will build a set of agendas that work for your business, and you will become so fluent at them you can put an effective agenda together in your sleep. Remember, in frontstage selling, put more attention on collaboration and less on one-way presentation, and incorporate into the agenda ideas we have discussed in this chapter. Start the meeting by posting the agenda in the chat.

Client:
Date:

Attendees:			
Name	**Position**	**Email**	**Phone**

Prep:

- Select pre-recorded videos to be shown during meeting.
- Choose SMEs to listen in/offer feedback.
- Ping attendees to remind them of meeting and provide a precursory agenda.
- Send meeting box out to all attendees (if applicable).
- Conduct pre-call research on all attendees—send LinkedIn invites prior to call.

Objectives:

- Discover potential opportunities to collaborate and produce mutual wins.
- Discuss referral program.
- Identify specific areas to improve upon:
  - Discuss potential solutions.
  - Discuss solution implementation.

Agenda:

1. Open/welcome
2. Introductions
3. Brief history of participants/company
4. Discuss objectives and vision
5. Discuss next steps:
   a. Better understand current set-up.
   b. Build a strategic plan of where we are and where we're going. Define different models based on company type.
   c. Decide financial inputs to bring the plan together.
   d. Build life-team members.
6. Closing comments

Here is a sample template to run an effective meeting. A downloadable version is available on our website: *www.masteringvirtualselling.com*.

Virtual Meeting Background. Here are samples of backgrounds that can help set the right stage in frontstage selling, depending on the effect you are looking for.

- ▶ Buyer's or seller's company logo
- ▶ Staged real background (e.g., school/sports team mascot, personal hobby, artwork, inspirations, awards)
- ▶ Blurred out non-descriptive actual background or virtual background

TIP: Leverage Key Resources. Be the first to ask subject-matter experts (SMEs) and executives to be on your call! Unlike in-person meetings where this would be an unusual move, inviting your company executive or SME to join you on a call is much easier—and more natural—in virtual selling, and there's no travel involved.

Pre-Recorded Videos. Here are types of prerecorded videos you can play in a frontstage meeting. They should be as short as possible, and you should **always** have these videos downloaded to your computer, versus streaming them live in the meeting. The combined bandwidth required for the virtual meeting and video streaming will put a risky level of burden on your network. Don't take the risk unless you absolutely have to.

▶ Customer-recorded videos. Ask your company to create a set of *customer testimonial videos* that you can choose from to play during the meeting. There is nothing better than having a third party validate the value of your solution(s). Video is a great way to convey that.

▶ **Ad hoc** executive videos. Ask your company to create a *two-minute recording from an executive* who has the most relevant message to share. To keep it authentic, it shouldn't be too polished. If you have the right infrastructure, an even better solution is to have your executive record an ad hoc video specifically for your meeting.

▶ SME videos. Instead of trying to convey complex information yourself, consider having your SME record and share that content. If what needs to be shared is long (e.g., greater than fifteen minutes), then send that ahead of time or even after the meeting, if it's more appropriate.

▶ "Breathing space" video. Consider a "breathing space" video that takes the eyes of the participants off you and gives you a few moments to clear your mind. It can be a "how-to" video, a video that further explains your subject, or even a funny video to lighten the tone of the meeting and/or make your point. Make sure it's short, as time is precious in frontstage.

Other Tips, Tools, and Techniques

Mutual Action Plan. Interactive content such as a mutual action plan is fantastic in facilitating next steps and is critical to moving the project forward, as well as keeping the audience engaged through collaboration. Below is an example. Having this document open during the meeting and sharing it on your screen allows the participants to work on this together with you.

[Company Name] – Allego: Mutual Action Plan

- Mutually agreed plan
- Communicate all changes

Owner	For	Action	When	Complete
		Executive presentation		
		Feedback from executive meeting		
		Vendor selection finalized		
		Discuss project scope(s) for proposal creation		
		Discuss implementation plan		
		Discuss and confirm optional add-ons		
		Proposal(s) shared and discussed		
		Initial proposal response		
		Proposal agreed upon		
		Walk through of order form and MSA (and DPA)		
		Legal review, redline initiated		
		IT / Security review initiated		
		IT review complete		
		All redlines complete		
		Routing for agreement execution		
		Agreement fully executed		
Allego		Allego access granted & virtual pre-work assigned*		
[Customer project team]		Allego virtual pre-work completed	Week 1	
Allego		Allego Customer Success Manager assigned	Week 1	
Project Team + Allego		Project Strategy Kick-Off Call	Week 2	
Project Team + Allego		Weekly status calls, implementation work	Week 3-8	

TIP: Calling Participants by Name or Quoting Them.

Dale Carnegie once said, "A person's name is to him or her the most important sound in any language." A sure way to get the audience engaged is to call them by name in the meeting. Calling them by name to ask questions and then repeating what they said or bringing their points to the forefront will help ensure individuals stay engaged!

TIP: Leverage the Chat Feature. We mentioned the best practice of posting the meeting agenda in the chat area at the beginning of any meeting. From that point forward, encourage the audience to ask questions in the chat window. In large meetings where time is compressed, you may need to have a separate stream of collaboration in the chat area. If you have team members joining you on the call, make sure the team members help monitor the chat area for any actions.

TIP: Screen Share *only* When Needed. Build rapport by maximizing (virtual) face-to-face time. Don't "park" the meeting where people are staring at a document when the conversation has moved elsewhere. Remember, you are always building rapport and earning trust.

TIP: Automating Note-Taking. Most modern virtual meeting tools can record the meeting. When you turn this on, with your buyer's permission, you automate the note-taking process so both parties can better focus on the conversation. There are also additional benefits in backstage selling that such recordings will offer, which we covered earlier. As we said, this form of recording is becoming increasingly more accepted across industries, and you want to take advantage of it.

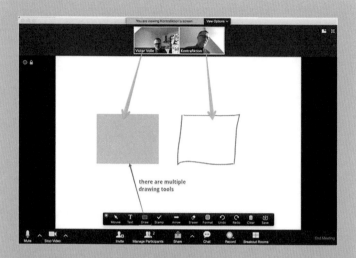

TIP: Leverage Virtual Whiteboards. There are numerous software applications available that simulate a physical whiteboard in a meeting. All major virtual meeting tools have this feature. To use it correctly, you need a stylus (a pencillike device) instead of a mouse, so there is a bit of setup required if you want to leverage this. In addition, our experience overwhelmingly confirms that the best practice is to utilize the *built-in* whiteboarding feature in your virtual meeting tool, versus using another virtual whiteboarding tool.

Technology Tips

Technology relevant to virtual selling is changing rapidly. Instead of listing information here that will quickly be obsolete, we have decided to keep updating the latest and greatest information on a dedicated website at *www.masteringvirtualselling.com.*

Frontstage Countdown Checklist

Just because you can book one frontstage meeting after another does not mean you should. Allowing buffer time between meetings allows you to check things off against a checklist to make sure you have everything ready before a call.

Here is a sample "Frontstage Countdown" checklist for a virtual meeting/call. We suggest you start with it but modify it over time to find one that fits your style and business. The most important idea we want to share with you is: *have a list*! There is a reason pilots do this on every flight, even though they have flown thousands of times. You will be more successful when the whole process is repeatable and consistent.

A Day or Two Before
▶ Send LinkedIn invites to attendees.
▶ Order food/drinks (if applicable).
▶ Make sure videos you may want to play are downloaded on your computer.
▶ Text the main contact buyer for a last-minute check, or even get on the phone for a few minutes to align if needed.

5 to 15 Minutes Before
▶ Close distracting apps on your desktop and turn off notifications.
▶ Preopen content/files or have links to them. (Make sure they don't time out.)
▶ List names of attendees.
▶ Ensure you have the agenda for the meeting ready and check time allotment to make sure you can cover all the topics.

continued on next page.

continued from previous page

- ▶ Pick a brand-oriented welcome background (or your own alternative background).
- ▶ Check your camera angle, microphone, and speaker (or your headset).
- ▶ Check your attire and how you look.
- ▶ Write down, print out, or have readily available on your *other* device (e.g., smartphone) the conference call-in number and key reference documents needed in the meeting—in case you need to revert to plan B and you need to dial in instead.
- ▶ When ready, get on the virtual meeting platform early and post the agenda bullets in the chat area.

During the Meeting

- ▶ Ask for permission to automate note-taking for everyone (i.e., record the call).
- ▶ Observe participants' backgrounds and find commonality or things to relate to.
- ▶ Manage energy by keeping it authentic, light, and interactive. Get others to talk. Use discovery questions and call on people with questions.
- ▶ Offload content if it will be too long to discuss, and keep a clear **follow-up** list to be processed afterward in backstage selling.
- ▶ Constantly be checking for background noise (yours especially), muting status, your own body language, and where your eyes are focusing.
- ▶ Constantly time-check the agenda.
- ▶ Constantly check how much time you are talking and who else needs to be talking more.

ENDNOTES

1 Morgan Wolan, "How to Read and Lead a Zoom Room," https://redvelvetevents.com/feed/how-to-read-and-lead-a-zoom-room.

BACKSTAGE
SELLING

chapter 4

"Amateur's practice until they can get it right;
masters practice until they can't get it wrong."
—Dan Sullivan

I magine wandering around the Magic Kingdom with your children and seeing their faces light up with wonder as they interact with Princess Jasmine or Winnie-the-Pooh. Much of the magic there is created by the characters as they mingle among the guests and delight children all over the park.

Sometimes, though, you may be looking for Cinderella or Captain Hook and find that they've disappeared. Actually, there's a set of secret tunnels at Disney World where the characters can pop in and out. The tunnel is the backstage area where they put on their makeup and costumes, and it's where the myriad details are handled—such as lights, sets, and props—that create the magical atmosphere in the frontstage area where the guests are.

Similarly, there is a backstage arena of virtual selling where the magic is created for the frontstage interaction with your buyer. The backstage part of virtual selling is where you are engaging with the buyer through a set of very effective asynchronous activities that don't require synchronous (frontstage) interaction.

What does it mean to be engaged with the buyer in asynchronous activities? Unlike collaborating through a meeting—virtual or in person—asynchronous activities are those that allow you to collaborate with your buyers independent of response time. The most primitive

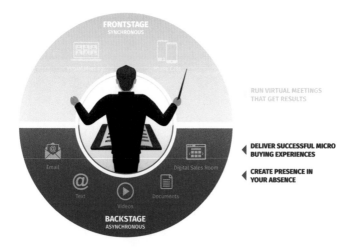

Backstage objectives

example is by postal mail. Another is by email, and another may be by text messaging (depending on the implicit understanding between you and your receiver that determines if and how you collaborate via text).

In this chapter we are going to drastically "amp up" our coverage of those backstage activities and establish their high essential value to the overall virtual-selling process and buyer experience.

BACKSTAGE CHALLENGES AND OPPORTUNITIES

Because of the challenges you face in the (synchronous) frontstage arena—the time limitation, the difficulty in building rapport, and the necessity of making every minute count—you need to offload to backstage many activities that you used to do in an in-person meeting, which will leave you more time in the frontstage virtual meetings to interact, facilitate, and collaborate.

Here are some of the challenges you are addressing in the backstage arena:

▶ Backstage activities are those you may need to do before the virtual meeting and often in a different—and sometimes more limited—form factor than they had been in frontstage.

For example, one-way presentations, especially long ones, should be offloaded to backstage whenever possible, where videos can be created and shared instead. Documents/collateral that are trackable can be sent electronically, and most contracts can now be signed electronically. Doing these well requires that you build "new muscles."

▶ Backstage activities are accomplished without engaging directly with the buyer, and there's a natural delay involved when you communicate indirectly (by text, email, snail mail, voice mail, etc.) and wait for a response. Consequently, you need to factor into account the delay and limit activities in the backstage to those that make sense. If they don't, you will have to move them to frontstage.

▶ Like spamming your buyers with emails, you can "overdo it" with too many backstage activities, especially if there are technologies to help make those activities as easy as pressing a few buttons. On the other hand, engaging in too few backstage activities leaves you with lost opportunities to

engage productively. So there is a Goldilocks
that needs to be achieved in backstage selling
provides just enough "presence" to stay top of mind.

And here are the unique opportunities related to the
backstage arena:

▶ Research shows that buyers are more receptive to a
robust backstage engagement than before, as they
would rather receive information, add their own
research, and digest it all at their own pace. In fact, 75
percent of B2B customers prefer remote sales
interactions over traditional face-to-face ones.[1] By not
requiring buyers to engage in a frontstage activity at a
specific time to
receive the
backstage
information, they
can choose to
consume the
information
whenever and
wherever they
want.

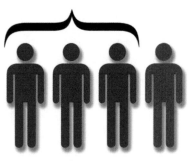

**75 PERCENT OF B2B CUSTOMERS PREFER
REMOTE SALES INTERACTIONS OVER
TRADITIONAL FACE-TO-FACE ONES.**

▶ Whatever content you create in the backstage can be
more polished because you are not doing it during live
interaction. And the quality will be higher since you
can incorporate editing. Think about how much more
you can do in an edited video versus talking live—it
can be shorter, more concise, and more engaging.

▶ Since you have more limited frontstage time with
your buyers, backstage is a way for you to continue

to be top of mind with your buyers before, after, and in between frontstage meetings. In essence, backstage activities help you "create presence in your absence" along the entire buying cycle.

Create presence in your absence.

▶ Thanks to technology in recent years, there is a whole arsenal of things you can do backstage that previously required sophisticated production to make them happen. That same technology also gives you insights that will help you analyze the situation and understand the interest level and interest areas of your buyers like never before.

▶ Unlike a virtual meeting in frontstage, where you have to perform in real time and do almost everything yourself, in backstage you can tap into your teammates and other company resources for help.

BING CROSBY: EARLY VIDEO PIONEER

BING CROSBY

The bestselling single of all time, according to the *Guinness Book of World Records*, is "White Christmas," sung by Bing Crosby. What most people don't know is that Crosby was also an early adopter of new technology—in this case, the condenser microphone—which he regarded as an instrument. The microphone allowed Crosby, with his bass/baritone voice, to sing in an informal, easygoing, and casual way. The primary appeal of this new approach was that the singer came across as someone who was in the room with you, sharing a joke or confiding a secret, as if he were someone you knew. Crosby influenced a whole generation of male singers who followed him, including Frank Sinatra, Dean Martin, Elvis Presley, and John Lennon.

Crosby learned to master this technology before most other artists, and much of what he learned relates to the frontstage communication strategies we've discussed so far. But his innovation didn't stop there. In the 1940s, he was the first major performer to prerecord his radio shows. With prerecording, he could control performing conditions and times and he could ad-lib and edit out mistakes. And by prerecording four shows a week, he could also spend more time on the golf course.

"Listen a lot and talk less. You can't learn anything when you're talking."
— Bing Crosby

It's easy to take for granted now the use and effectiveness of recording content for use "backstage." Crosby's radio career took a significant turn in 1945 when he clashed with NBC over his insistence that he be allowed to prerecord his radio shows. Both the network and the sponsors were adamantly opposed to Crosby's prerecording. They argued that the public would not stand for "canned" radio broadcasts. Crosby used his clout, both professional and financial, for innovations in audio. He said, "By using tape, I could do a thirty-five or forty-minute show, then edit it down to the twenty-six or twenty-seven minutes the program ran. This allowed us to take out jokes, gags, or situations that didn't play well and finish with only the 'prime meat' of the show, the solid stuff that plays big."

Crosby's story demonstrates that there are always people who resist new technologies and want to keep things the way they were. In addition to his work as an artist, he also became a successful entrepreneur, and his company, Bing Crosby Enterprises, helped finance the development of video tape and showed the world the first video tape recording on November 11, 1951. The strategies we are recommending for using prerecorded content have been building ever since Crosby first introduced video tapes.[2]

GOALS OF BACKSTAGE SELLING

1. **Create a Winning Experience for Your Buyers**
   Understanding what buying stage your buyer is in is critical for all backstage activities. One of the biggest mistakes sellers make is not being aligned with their buyers and, as a result, wasting precious opportunities

sending irrelevant content or trying
to make a decision when they're not
especially true when it comes to com[

For example, it's a mistake to try to push people
to buy something when they're still in the research
phase; they're just not ready to do it yet. If they
are interested in understanding the difference
between the options that are available, focus on
finding the best report that explains that. That
shows you understand where they are and that you
are just giving them helpful information.

If you want to be a master virtual seller, you must
get into your buyers' heads so you can support
them, across both frontstage and backstage, in
whatever buying stage they are in. Based on
everything you know about the buyers from
your research and the interaction you've had in
frontstage, you should have a strong sense of what
stage they are in at all times.

A huge part of backstage is providing your
buyers with whatever content would give them
the context to progress favorably along their
buying process. Rather than thinking about how
much information or product you can pump to
your buyers, approach it from their perspective.
Remember, your job as the seller is to help the
buyer. If you're talking to the full decision maker,
ask, *What content do I need to give my buyer to help him
or her make a decision?* Or ask the person directly,
"How can I be most helpful?" or "What can I do
to save you time?" Once you know what the buyer

needs, an effective backstage activity could involve sending a link and saying, "If you have time, you may want to watch this video. It answers the question you had in our last call."

Remember, companies don't buy; people do. If there are other stakeholders involved in the decision making, your goal is to make it as easy as possible for the buyer to get a yes from each one. For example, you may have a tool the buyer could use at an internal meeting, such as a summary of the most popular features of your product and why it's superior to other alternatives. And to save the buyer time, you may want to send that summary in both a PowerPoint format and a one-pager.

Companies don't buy, people do.

We can't stress enough that the most important thing is to match the right content with the buying stage they're in—not just the last stage of the cycle, which is the final decision. They must first get to the point where they can confidently say yes and can defend that decision. Then when the boss asks, "Why are you selecting this vendor? Have you thought of X, Y, or Z?" the buyer is prepared with an informed response.

2. **Earn Trust and Build Your Buyer's Confidence**
   Your overall goal is to instill confidence in your buyers that you are the right partner for them. Rapport building is not just an important part of the frontstage event; assuming you are the vendor

of choice, it's also important that you leverage backstage interactions to continue to build rapport and trust. So how do you reinforce that in backstage selling? Examples of backstage content include:

▶ third-party independent collateral, such as a respected analyst's report on the market space;

▶ a research document covering the solution areas of interest;

▶ testimonials of other customers very similar to your buyer;

▶ information about your company and/or a video of your CEO or other executives—to build trust in your company as well as yourself;

▶ a video of yourself answering a question or directing the buyer to information they may need.

It's important that you leverage backstage interactions to continue to build rapport and trust.

STRATEGY OF BACKSTAGE SELLING

1. **Create Successful Micro Buying Experiences**
   The buyer's journey is made up of a series of micro buying experiences, which is the cycle of actual collaboration that is taking place at any given time. For example, you may have just finished a meeting with a buyer, and you have another meeting planned for next week. These two meetings are two micro buying experiences

that you need to orchestrate successfully. Backstage selling helps generate highly effective experiences around a virtual meeting by pre-engaging the audience before the meeting *and* post-engaging the attendees after the meeting.

Backstage selling helps generate highly effective experiences around a virtual meeting by pre-engaging the audience before the meeting **and** *post-engaging the attendees after the meeting.*

These pre- and post-meeting backstage activities, together with frontstage, make up a complete micro buying experience, all done sequentially and for the benefit of the buyer's needs at a specific moment.

For example, before a meeting, a backstage activity may be to send a video of you sharing with attendees the agenda for the upcoming meeting. Or you may send them background content that may be pertinent. After the meeting, you may want to send them a quick thank-you video and list what was decided and what the next steps are. When done right, these activities build rapport and trust and will result in your coming across as someone who is helpful. There is a list of examples of how to do this in the backstage arsenal shown at the end of this chapter. Making the best possible use of them will allow you to save time, build rapport, and be better engaged on the frontstage, which helps you create a superior buyer experience.

Here's a great example: A large financial service company was looking for a way to differentiate their salespeople. Kent, one of the top B2B sellers, decided to use the power of video to differentiate his approach. He knew there were four other vendors who would be conducting virtual meetings with the prospective client. In the past, he had just sent a brief email with a bullet-pointed agenda. This time he sent a short video from the Atlanta Braves baseball stadium on a day when a special event was happening to honor the late Hank Aaron. Using his cell phone, he recorded a message that tied into Hank Aaron's being an all-star, explaining how he wanted to help this prospect be an all-star for its employees. He sent this sixty-second video along with the agenda, and the response he received was totally unexpected. He said, "In the past, these calls had always started in a very professional manner that made it hard to build any rapport, and we had to immediately get down to business. This time, as soon as I joined the virtual call, people started asking me about the game and telling me they watched the video." The new approach created a totally different response on the call and led to Kent's being chosen as a finalist—one of two firms chosen out of five. In his final presentation, he explained how he used video to communicate with employees and how he had adapted to the world of virtual communication. In a close race, a small thing can make a big difference. Kent ended up winning the deal and was told afterward by the buyer that the video he sent helped set him apart because no one else had done that.

MICRO BUYING EXPERIENCE

BEFORE	DURING	AFTER
• Video Intro	• Agenda in Chat	• Thank You Email/Video
• Agenda	• Intro/Build Trust	• Summarize Key Points
• LinkedIn Bios	• Discovery	• Links to Content
	• Record Call	• Share Recording

Use Templates to Create Strong Pre/Post-Meeting Engagements

Using templates will save you time and create a better experience for your buyers. For example, Tony sends a meeting outline template to participants before each meeting that includes the objectives, the agenda, and a list of the people in attendance, including their contact information. This template can mentally prepare people to be ready to focus during the frontstage time. You should consider creating a sixty-second video of yourself talking or doing a voiceover on a slide of yourself, explaining the objectives and the agenda. (Be creative when possible, as Kent was in the story we told above.) In the video you can also encourage people to think about items they may want to review or discuss beforehand and/or bring to the table in the live frontstage arena.

After a meeting, follow up with a thank-you video and recap the action items. Also remind the buyers of the key points you were trying to convey during the meeting as well as the fact that you are a resource for *them* in this process. "Templatizing" your ⓔ approach will help you home in on what works for your company and your own authentic style. But the key is to repeat and get fluent and efficient at this. You can see additional examples of templates in the backstage arsenal at the end of this chapter.

2. Create Presence in Your Absence

In addition to creating strong micro buying experiences, in between these meetings, you will have an opportunity to do some backstage selling and "create presence in your absence" by sharing useful information to the buyers.

"Create presence in your absence" in between micro buying experiences by sharing useful information to the buyers in backstage selling.

This is the process of coordinating backstage activities that help nurture the buying process favorably forward. This content can be used over and over again by you and your peers on your sales team. Examples could include:

Research

▶ content to help anchor the overall vision and to help buyers with their research (i.e., industry analyst reports, third-party SMEs, etc.);

▶ content that highlights specific products or services that are most relevant to the buyer;

content that identifies relevant differentiation
(i.e., analyst's reports or media coverage on why
certain features matter for specific products);

▶ customer testimonials;

▶ executive/SME videos tailored to add value
and build trust at specific stages.

During the research stage, you're not trying to close
the sale; you're just dripping information to the buyer
to the point where they are ready to ask you questions
or engage. This content will help you nurture that
relationship over time until you reach that point
of readiness when things start to get serious.

KEY ELEMENTS FOR TACKLING BACKSTAGE SELLING

1. **Focus on Content That's Both Effective and Easy**

   We mentioned the foundation of backstage selling
   is to keep asking the key question, *Am I adding
   value to the buyer?* Equally (if not more) important
   is the "form factor" of the content. Are you
   making it *easy* for the buyer? For example:

   ▶ Don't send a ten-page document if you can help it!

   ▶ If you are sharing videos, remember that the
   shorter, the better. According to AdAge, "If
   you have not fully engaged your audience
   after the first 30 seconds, you've likely lost
   33% of your viewers, and after one minute,
   45% of viewers have stopped watching."[3]

   ▶ If you must send a dense document, send it with
   a voiceover or a video explaining what it is and

why the buyer should invest time reading it. Also explain the best way for the buyer to efficiently get the gist of the document's content.

▶ Think about "dripping" information over time to "choreograph" the reveal of coveted information. This will not only make each content item easier to consume, but it will also increase the frequency of interactions, which builds rapport and trust.

▶ Link additional relevant content before and after meetings to create clarity and engagement (as discussed earlier).

▶ If you are creating videos, make sure you are not creating a raw video on an iPhone and sending it to your client via email. (Three minutes can be as much as 500MB in size!). Use tools that are dedicated to making these videos work.

▶ There are sales-enablement tools today that allow you to create and send not just documents and videos but interactive content as well. As an example, Allego's sales-enablement platform allows for this type of content creation. This is content that can embed actions the buyer can take, such as scheduling a meeting on a calendar, taking a poll of what participants are interested in for the upcoming meeting, or taking a fun or clarifying quiz. It can also embed a personalized video with documents and link to other content.

▶ Leverage technologies that can track over time what content works the best at what stage to optimize effectiveness.

Make it easy for the buyer by being aware of the "form factor" of the content you are sending them.

We share more in the backstage arsenal about other types of content you can send besides documents and videos.

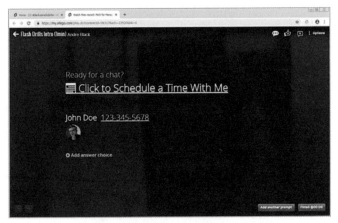

Example of interactive content in your
video to schedule a meeting

"The medium is the message."
—Marshall McLuhan

Through these examples, you can see that we put a heavy emphasis on video content. Video, especially one with your face on it—is an exceptionally strong form factor. For one thing, video is much easier for the buyer to consume in many settings than documents. (Look how popular YouTube is! According to research,

YouTube has more than two billion logged-in monthly users, and people watch more than a billion hours of video on YouTube every day.[4]) For another, showing your face makes a more personal connection across various parts of virtually selling, where the lack of person-to-person connection can be a barrier to success.

Now, one important thing to remember is that you should think, "YouTube, not Hollywood" when it comes to creating a video. Here's what we mean: To make this work, you really don't have time to create professional-looking and polished videos that will be used just once! Marketing may be able to invest in a high-quality video for you if it's going to be reused as a selling tool (e.g., a short video of your CEO). However, when it comes to backstage selling where you are trying to "create presence in your absence" with your buyer, YouTube quality is just fine. Our research shows that creating an ad hoc video of you helping the client solve his or her problems builds strong rapport and conveys a level of authenticity that no polished video can deliver. So have confidence that an ad hoc video from you will be effective because it shows you are a human being, you're a helpful partner to your buyer, and you're doing your job well.

Think, "YouTube, not Hollywood" when it comes to creating a video.

As an example, Mark reached out to the salesperson who covers the Allego account for Zoom. He was having trouble setting up Zoom to use a professional microphone, and he had a specific question about it. In less than ten minutes, Mark's salesperson, Jessie, responded with an email that included a short video capturing Jessie's screen and showing him exactly how to navigate to the box he needed to select. This saved both Mark and Jessie time, as there was no need for a phone call, and it was much easier to *see* how to do this versus *hearing* how to do it.

We have a more extensive list on our website than what's shared here in our backstage arsenal.

2. The Difference Is You!

You can leverage the resources you have in the backstage arena to maximize the outcome. Since you have more time to react in backstage, you can beef up what you need to know with "just-in-time learning" (versus having to remember everything while you are in front of the buyer). Think of the last time you needed to fix something in your house. What did you do? You probably looked up your project on YouTube to learn what you needed to do—just in time! It's the same here. You are working backstage now and don't have to know everything in real time for a frontstage meeting. As a result, you have time to learn things on the fly, ask for help, and use in-house collaboration tools (e.g., asynchronous brainstorming, explained in the gray bar below) to engage SMEs to help produce content that will enhance the buyer's experience.

Asynchronous Brainstormin

A very common sales problem happens when a deal is "stuck" or classified "code red," or when the buyer's problem at hand needs to be solved with the help of multiple people in your organization. The bigger the problem, the more people (and more senior people) you need. To compound the challenge, these situations tend to be highly time sensitive and require immediate actions. Now, have you ever tried to get a meeting of, say, five very busy people (perhaps including a CXO) in a meeting with two days' notice? You see the problem: scheduling such a meeting on the calendar is nearly impossible in real life.

If the problem requires only one or two people to "make a call" and no drawn-out brainstorming or back-and-forth discussion is needed, you may be able to resolve the problem through email or a quick phone call or two. But if the problem requires a team of people to have a robust dialogue or brainstorm the problem, your best bet is to leverage tools that are now available to help you brainstorm—*asynchronously*.

Here's how it works: Start with recording a video (perhaps voiceover a PowerPoint slide or two) and articulate the core issues, where you need help, and the options you are aware of. Then share this video with the key people you need input from. The tool allows each individual to respond at their own time (with "inline" voice recording, text, or video feedback), enabling a "threaded discussion" at different points in time on the video and thereby simulating a brainstorming—but doing so asynchronously, back and forth—that you can't get effectively from email.

Example of inline feedback allowing backstage collaboration

In essence, it is much easier for busy people who may be able to help you to consume a video (and it's quicker for you than writing a long email!). By allowing them to participate and provide input when they have time, you are able to overcome the calendaring problem in trying to set up a meeting in short order (which is nearly impossible to do). Now, is this better than having all participants in a live (synchronous) meeting? No. Is it better than the alternative of not having their help? Infinitely.

The same approach also can help you gain confidence in preparing for an important meeting by recording what you are going to say and sending it to your sales managers, trusted peers, or SMEs to provide feedback and help you polish your messaging. We have also seen companies where frontline sales managers require new sellers to record and share videos for the first few important meetings beforehand—to ensure they get the benefit of feedback and coaching before they go frontstage.

3. Leverage Technology

Similar to frontstage selling where virtual meeting technology is essential, backstage selling is also grounded in an important set of technologies. We mentioned this in passing earlier, but let's dig in more here.

Let's summarize some of the key capabilities that should be considered to support backstage selling:

▶ Ability to send relevant and *trackable* content via email to buyers. Best-in-class companies prebuild "playbooks" that help sellers determine, among the voluminous possible content each buyer may be interested in, which content may be the most effective. This is based on statistics collected (and some AI magic) from actions of past similar buyers. It is possible because there is now an ability to record what a person views electronically. Now, this may seem somewhat eerie, but understand that this is now standard among many industries, and it includes everything you do in your personal life as well! Some industries (and countries) require disclosure that you are tracking, so make sure your compliance officers sign off on this type of usage. (See the gray sidebar on B2B tracking and privacy.)

▶ Ability to generate ad hoc *trackable* personalized videos. On the surface, sending a video of you talking to your buyer may not sound like a big deal. (Everyone has a smartphone and can do that.) In reality, it's a lot more involved than that. For one thing, videos are big files! If you send a five-minute video to your client, it may be anywhere from 50 MB to 450 MB in size! Even if it gets through their corporate email system, do you think your client appreciates your spamming their inbox with these huge files? Also, you have no idea if these videos are interesting to your buyer. Instead, it's best to invest in a sales-enablement capability that allows you to generate an ad hoc video, optimized for speed and ease, that you can send to your buyer as a link—similar to how people access YouTube videos. This sales enablement capability also allows you to track whether they have any interest. Since you have less face-to-face opportunities, having the ability to efficiently and effectively send these personalized videos *at key moments* within the buying process is critical to backstage selling success. Companies that have this capability today have a massive advantage over their competitors!

Companies that have the capability to generate ad hoc **trackable** *personalized videos today have a massive advantage over their competitors!*

▶ Ability to generate highly effective presentations. We mentioned that in virtual selling, it's important to consider offloading one-way presentations from frontstage virtual meetings to backstage. But how do you do that? There are technologies now that allow individual sellers, with a few clicks, to generate specific video recordings of themselves doing slide presentations, using voiceover, which can then be sent to buyers. There are many variations of this type of video-based presentation (check out our list of examples in our backstage arsenal), such as a voiceover PowerPoint presentation (with or without your face), or a screen recording of a software demo. Sharing content this way allows you to create the videos ahead of time, which means you can correct mistakes. (But make sure you don't waste time on perfection here.) The content, if it is generic, can also be reused in future meetings for other buyers, which saves you time. Having this type of technology and being fluent at it will make you feel like the only gun slinger in a gunfight, where all your competitors just bring knives.

► Ability to generate content that allows buyers
to interact with you. Sometimes, you just need
to know before a meeting what topics are
most interesting among the, say, fifteen people
who will be on a call. If you try to mass email
them, you are only going to hear feedback
from a couple of them. Instead, imagine
running a small poll to get their thoughts.
What if you could email your buyer a video
recording of you summarizing the call you
just had, and the video contained a spot where
you could get feedback from the buyer or even
have them select the next meeting date—and
that meeting would show up "automagically"
on both your calendars? We called this
interactive content, and it serves a useful role in
enriching asynchronous collaboration between
buyers and sellers and helping the entire
buying process be more productive.

► Ability to automatically take notes in
frontstage virtual meetings so you can review
them backstage. As we said, today every
virtual meeting tool allows you to record the
call (with the buyer's permission). What if
you had a person in every meeting who could
transcribe the entire conversation? You would
no longer need to frantically try to remember
what you needed to say and do during a call
while simultaneously trying to listen and
take notes on what your buyers are saying.
There are technologies that can transcribe the

call for you once the call is recorded, which allows you to review, search, analyze, and spot weaknesses (e.g., are you talking too much?) or opportunities (notice keywords used by the buyer), as well as improve your next call. The AI-based technologies here are not 100 percent perfect, but they are becoming more amazing. (Do you have an Alexa at home?) Recording your calls will help you perform better frontstage because it allows you to listen more completely; but more importantly, it allows you to "rewind the tape" and *really* listen to your buyers—backstage.

Recording your calls helps you listen more completely, and, more importantly, it allows you to "rewind the tape" to really hear what your buyers are saying.

▶ Ability to *centralize* the exchange of content and collaboration in an easy-to-find "place" digitally. In a typical B2B buyer-seller engagement, there are dozens and even upwards of hundreds of email exchanges, back and forth, between the seller and multiple people representing the buying company. It's extremely difficult for buyers or sellers to keep track of the thread of dialogues throughout the buying experience. A new capability that is emerging in support of backstage virtual selling allows the seller to orchestrate a "digital place" to house all the back-and-forth dialog and content, with the primary objective of making the buyer's journey better. But of course it also adds to the seller's ability to better organize information, track buyers' interest level and what they are doing, and efficiently engage individual buyers throughout the journey. There are several names for these "digital places"—**digital sales rooms (DSRs)**, deal rooms, or even virtual sales rooms—but the functionality is the same. For simplicity, we'll call this concept a DSR. Think of it as a dedicated website on steroids— one that is created *just* for this one buyer for this one buying journey with you. It may include a personal welcome video from you and a list of relevant research or testimonials relevant to the buyer, threaded chat and discussions to help answer questions, and recordings of previous meetings so everyone is on the same page. Remember, there is tremendous value in curating content for your buyers to save them time. For example, you could make a short video that acts as a buyer's "**Sherpa guide**" that has embedded links where you provide content and meaning.

Master sellers understand the power of curating relevant content to save their buyers' time.

Andre Black, Allego's chief product officer, recently recorded a welcome video for use in a DSR for a prospect, where he explained the resources that were available in the DSR. He also explained how this location could act as a centralized hub for collaboration between the Allego team and the prospect throughout the buying cycle. Providing a short welcome video is like meeting a guest at your front door and walking them into your business.

00:01 About this Digital Sales Room

Andre Black, Allego's chief product officer, recently recorded a welcome video for use in a DSR for a prospect

Technology is a fast-evolving space. We have touched on some of the state-of-the-art technologies we see being used in backstage virtual selling, but improvements are happening all the time. So instead of treating what we are sharing here as static, make sure you check out the associated website we have created to keep you up to date on technologies that are evolving as well as the information/best practices associated with their usage: *www.masteringvirtualselling.com*.

What you need to know about privacy laws

Most websites collect information about their users that has either been submitted by the users or collected automatically via cookies and other technologies. Business owners need information to deliver their products, advertise their services, communicate with customers and prospective customers, and improve their website functionality. Customers and visitors to your site are understandably concerned about what happens to their personal information when visiting a website—how it is stored, who has access to it, and what safeguards are in place to protect their privacy.

Virtually every country has enacted some sort of data privacy laws to regulate how information is collected, how data subjects are informed, and what control data subjects have over their information once it is transferred. Failure to follow applicable data privacy may lead to fines, lawsuits, and even prohibition of a site's use in certain jurisdictions. Navigating these laws and regulations can be daunting, but all website operators should be familiar with data privacy laws that affect their users. Having an understanding of the laws that govern the geography where you do business will go a long way toward avoiding an unnecessary problem. The solution could be as simple as making sure your customers know what you are doing with their data and consent to it.

The good news is, when it comes to leveraging trackable content, it is already widespread and frankly accepted as standard in most industries, so you don't have to stand out on the bleeding edge on this. As long as you are adding value to your buyers, they will opt into virtual collaboration because of its convenience and continue to build a strong dialogue based on mutual value and trust.

PULLING IT ALL TOGETHER

There are certain activities a seller does backstage before a live meeting, and there are other activities the seller does to prepare to conduct the live meeting itself, in frontstage. There are also certain activities the seller does after the meeting. These activities before, during, and after the virtual meeting, collectively, are called a micro buying experience. The buying process is made up of a number of micro buying experiences for B2B software sales—possibly as many as seven to ten in order to get from the first call all the way to the negotiation call or closing the deal.

In between the individual micro buying experiences is an opportunity we call "**creating presence in your absence**," which is something all the great brands do. That's why you see the Nike "Swoosh" logo or Coca Cola signs everywhere—it's their way of continually reminding you about their brand (keeping it top of mind), even when you're not using the product.

We're suggesting that the same logic and the same marketing best practices also apply to you, as an individual seller. And to that end, we want to bring to your awareness the notion of creating presence in your absence and give you some examples in the case study below of how to do this. What you need to remember is that your selling world is made up of a micro buying experience that gets repeated over time and that you need to make a conscious effort to create presence in your absence in between meetings.

CASE STUDY NO. 2: A MICRO BUYING EXPERIENCE

Background

Tim, an executive sponsor from a large medical device company, asked Jake, an Allego salesperson, to help facilitate an internal virtual roundtable meeting with fifteen of his peers. These were all executives from other divisions in the company who were unfamiliar with the platform. The purpose of the meeting was to describe how the sponsor's division was using Allego's sales-enablement platform and explain specific use cases that would be relevant across the enterprise.

Backstage (Pre-Meeting)

1. In advance of the meeting, Jake met with Tim to discuss objectives, potential objectives, and the people who would be invited.

2. Following this meeting, Tim sent an email invitation that included a sixty-second video message with an embedded agenda and explained the purpose of the meeting, along with a statement explaining why those invited would benefit from

attending. The email included the LinkedIn screenshots of each participant, which was designed to streamline introductions and help these peers quickly understand who else would be attending.

3. Tim created a slide deck after collaborating with Jake in advance of the meeting. As a result of the brainstorming, Tim was able to reduce the key messages they wanted to share into just five slides.

4. Jake and Tim had a pre-call rehearsal to ensure that all the needed videos and collateral were organized, downloaded, and ready to share in the presentation. This rehearsal also served to clarify how much time Tim and Jake would be talking versus how much time would be available for discussion and questions.

Frontstage (Meeting)

Before the call, Jake closed all extraneous web browsers and tabs and made sure his desktop was clean and all materials were easily accessible. Jake also ran through his tried and true pre-call frontstage countdown checklist, like an experienced pilot does before flying his plane.

Because Jake had scheduled gaps between meetings, he was able to join the virtual meeting five minutes before the scheduled start time, along with the executive sponsor.

Jake initiated the call recording after he received approval from the executive sponsor, which was signified by a flashing red icon on the screen and automatically announced as each participant joined the call.

As participants joined the call, Jake made sure to say hello and start the rapport-building process.

At the scheduled meeting time, Jake welcomed everyone, and Tim set the stage for the call; then Jake began sharing his screen.

During the presentation he used **targeted polling** to call on people by name and get them engaged in the conversation.

As planned, Tim reviewed the five slides, and then Jake shared a two-minute video that demonstrated a specific example of how Tim's division was using video to interact with medical professionals.

This sparked a wide-ranging conversation about different use cases that were applicable across different divisions.

Jake monitored the time throughout the call and reminded everyone with statements such as, "In our remaining ten minutes, here is what we'd like to accomplish."

Before the call ended, one of the executives said he liked the way Tim described a use case during this call but could not remember exactly what was said. Jake offered to send a recorded snippet to the group with this content from the call recording and added this to his backstage follow-up list.

After the Q&A and with five minutes remaining, Jake recapped the key action items from this call, along with the next steps. The call ended on time.

Backstage (Post Meeting)

Following the call, Jake texted Tim to get feedback. Tim replied via text and stated, "The meeting hit the mark." Tim said he believed there were at least three executives on the call who needed immediate follow-up and that Jake should reach out to them directly.

Jake created and sent out (via email) a link to a one-minute personalized video of himself, which included:

▶ a thank-you to the participants and a summary of the key takeaways and discussion points; embedded within the video was the PDF of the PowerPoint presentation and the two-minute snippet from the call featuring the content that was requested; and

▶ a summary of action items and next steps.

Backstage (Continue to Nurture and Create Presence)

In the weeks since the call, Jake has continued to provide support to the customer, as more people have become interested in Allego. After the third email dialogue with several key people, Jake decided to set up a DSR to keep everything in one virtual place for this opportunity and invited a handful of key people from the buying organization to access it.

Since then, Jake has run a few more virtual meetings to collaborate and understand the right solution that fits the problem the company is looking to solve, using the tried and true pre/during/post meeting "micro buying experience" format. Over a period of weeks, the DSR served as a virtual place to collaborate and share vital content, including email messages and recorded phone calls, and act as a location to post answers to key questions among all the participants. To help buyers navigate their understanding of solution options, Jake posted past content that had been shared as well as subsequent recordings (and their transcribed notes) of key brainstorming meetings. He also included a library of material that Jake's marketing organization had created specifically for the medical device industry. All future dialogue, sharing of content, and collaboration through chat will be supported by the dedicated DSR, which will simplify everyone's life.

As the executive sponsor for this customer, it was a pleasure for Yuchun to watch Jake orchestrate all the calls, shared content, and DSR activities. The feedback across the board was positive, not only in terms of more interest in learning about the Allego platform for other divisions but also in serving as a best-practice example of a great buying experience. It showed how virtual selling that incorporates frontstage and backstage techniques could actually be more valuable than an in-person selling approach.

Jake's confidence was evident in his post-sale win report debriefing to the Allego sales team, via a video recording, which explained the process and some of the key reasons why he was successful with this expansion. He made the point to his peers that it is unlikely he would have been able to get all of these executives, from multiple divisions, located around the globe, in one place for the roundtable meeting if he had been selling in person. His message ended by saying that when this virtual selling experiment started, he was skeptical, but he now understands why the virtual approach can make sellers more productive than they were in the past. He ended by saying that just before the pandemic, the last time he visited a client, his return flight was delayed by five hours. The virtual approach has not only helped him do more meetings that were relevant to his buyers; more importantly, it has given him more time with his wife and new baby versus being stuck in an airport waiting for a delayed flight.

VIRTUAL SELLING TIMELINE

FRONTSTAGE
Synchronous Collaboration

Timeline

BACKSTAGE
Asynchronous Collaboration

Micro Buying Experience

MEETING #1

- Agenda (in Chat)
- Intro, build trust
- Discovery
- Record call

- Video intro
- Agenda
- LinkedIn Bios

- Send thank you email/video
- Summarize key points & actions
- LinkedIn Bios

Create Presence in Your Absence

- Solution vision guide
- Relevant collateral
- Whitepapers

- Customer testimonial
- Executive video

- Expert opinions
- Analyst reports

Micro Buying Experience

MEETING #2

- Agenda (in Chat)
- Problem solving
- Collaboration
- Record call (& share)

- Video intro
- Agenda
- Key questions to answer

- Buy (virtual) lunch!

- Thanks!
- Summarize key actions
- Links to useful content

continued on next page

VIRTUAL SELLING TIMELINE

continued from previous page

FRONTSTAGE	**BACKSTAGE**
Synchronous Collaboration	*Asynchronous Collaboration*

Timeline

Micro Buying Experience

MEETING #3

- Prep call on next major solution presentation meeting
- Record call (& share)

- Video intro
- Agenda
- Key questions to answer

- Thanks!
- Summarize key points
- Links to useful content

Create Presence in Your Absence

- Product/services collateral
- Differentiation
- Whitepapers

- Evaluation criteria
- Analyst reports

- Invite buyers to Digital Sales Room
- Share meeting recording in Digital Sales Room

- Expert opinions
- Analyst reports

Micro Buying Experience

MEETING #4

- Pricing, terms, negotiation
- Collaboration, Q&A
- Record call (& share)

- Send agenda
- Key things to expect

Backstage Arsenal

Below is a list of content types, contact strategy, and various tips we have seen success with when incorporated into backstage selling. They include new ways to think about communicating with buyers when you are not meeting them in virtual meetings (or in person).

General Approach
Bite-Sized Content. It's very important that you send only bite-sized videos and one- to two-page documents. Anything longer will deteriorate the buyer's engagement level.
Let Buyers Determine Appropriate Frequency. When sending content (emails, videos, documents), always make sure your content is value-add and relevant to the buyer, and make sure they are not too frequent. Let your buyer lead the level of "back and forth," and always ask to see if the level you are on is okay. You have only a few shots at sending irrelevant content before your buyer mentally opts out of your backstage effort. So treat communication with care.
Dripping Content. Think about dripping relevant content over time to stretch out the number of times you are connecting virtually with your buyer. This is far superior to sending a burst of content that creates short-lived interactions; the volume will only serve to overwhelm your buyer, and they will likely not absorb everything you send.
Move Email Back-and-Forth to a Digital Sales Room (DSR). Once the buyer is truly engaged and you are a trusted party in the buying process, engage the buyer through a DSR to help organize content and make collaboration easy for everyone.

Activate Content with Personalized Explanation. Instead of just sending a document or a white paper to the buyer, also send a video of yourself explaining what the white paper or document is. (Ideally, use a technology that embeds the white paper and the document together to provide a multimedia experience.) By providing context explaining why the document or white paper is useful or how it applies to the project at hand, the buyer will be more interested, and the content will be much more effective.

Trackable Content. Make sure all content shared allows you visibility to the buyers' engagement level. This is one of the most important parts of backstage selling because it can provide you insights into the buyer's true interest level and potentially the scope of exposure of the project throughout the buyer's organization. When there is activity, you can set this content up to alert you.

External Viewer Activity

Tracking Label	Content Item / Author / Share Date	Viewer	Viewer's Visit #	Visit Start	Est. % Viewed	Responses Posted	Downloa
		Sales Demos					
CMS Talk Track	Russ Junkins HiTech Demo Mgr CMS Talk Track 12/28/2020 9:21 AM	Brian Sullivan, Allego	1	12/28/2020 11:13 AM	58%		0
		Brian Sullivan, Allego	2	12/28/2020 1:06 PM	5%		0
Demo prep	Russ Junkins HiTech Demo Mgr Demo Prep 3/31/2021 2:16 PM	Anonymous user [174.192.8.193, 64.262.157149]	1	3/31/2021 4:30 PM	83%		0
		Allego Admin, HCL Technologies	1	3/31/2021 9:02 PM	87%		0
		Maureen Beattie, Allego	1	3/31/2021 6:35 PM	19%		0
		Russ Jenkins HiTech Demo Mgr, Allego Sales Demos	1	3/31/2021 2:23 PM	55%		0
		Tony Jones, Allego	1	3/31/2021 4:39 PM	0%		0
		Tony Jones, Allego	2	3/31/2021 4:39 PM	100%		0
Demo Prep		Kaitlyn Champlin	1	2/11/2021	100%		0

Example of external viewing report from Allego

TIP: Remind your buyers that they can speed up the video you send. Most people talk slow enough that speeding up their recording by 25 to 50 percent makes it easier to absorb and saves time. It's like having the ability to skip TV commercials, and once your buyers are used to this feature, they will never go back to playing a video at the regular speed like they have to do with videos from your competitors.

Example of changing the playback speed

Micro Buying Experience

One of the most important parts of backstage selling is to properly bookend frontstage activities to form compelling micro buying experiences. Below is a template for how to do that.

Pre-Meeting
Pre-Meeting Personalized Video. Send a personalized video of yourself, casual and authentic, saying how you are looking forward to the upcoming meeting and talking about key items you will be discussing. Shoot for YouTube, not Hollywood, quality to add authenticity and optimize your time.
Stage-Setting Content. Send vision-setting content that can be summarized in a two-minute video to set the vision for how you engage your client, how to think about the problem at hand, where you can help, and so forth. Note that this can be part of your personalized video, a video from an executive or SME from your company, or a one- to two-page document.

Clarify Meeting Topics Through Polls. If this is a meeting catering to several people who potentially have different needs, or if there is a set of choices for what you can discuss during the meeting, consider sending a quick poll to the audience to help you rank order the topics and design a productive agenda. There are tools that allow a seller to do this with only a few clicks.

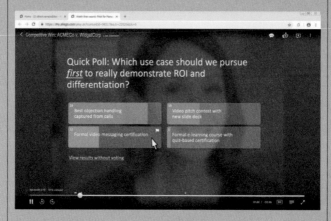

Example of quick poll from Allego

Post-Meeting

Post-Meeting Personalized Video. Record and send a video of yourself to all participants, thanking all for the opportunity to hold the meeting, summarizing the key points you want them to take away from the meeting, and listing key action items and follow-throughs.

Content Follow-Ups. Send videos or documents that cover deeper elements of what was discussed and material you promised to follow up on. Leverage content created by others for you when necessary.

Call Recording. Send the recording of the meeting or clips of important parts to the participants. Ideally, once your buyer is highly engaged with you, this call recording, as well as other pre/post-meeting content, is shared via the DSR, driving easier and more visible interactions for all.

Create Presence in Your Absence

Aside from creating micro buying experiences, the other important role of backstage selling is to continue to engage the buyer in between frontstage meetings. Below are activities that work.

Create Presence in Your Absence
Buyer Stage Drives Content to Be Shared. Match content to the stage your buyer is in (e.g., sending research papers, analyst reports, buyer ratings, or vision documents when the buyer is still in the research and problem-definition stage). Ideally, your company has playbooks of content ready as options for you to consider sharing. When possible, and especially for opportunities that are further along, a seller should use judgment to ensure the content being shared is relevant to the buyer, versus just relying on an automated outreach campaign. Remember, relevancy is key.
Match Content to Buyers. Any time you run across something newsworthy or that is of interest, think through all the buyers who may benefit from this content. Note that this can be content that either relates to the project or is just personal; consider it a potential opportunity to share with the buyer to build rapport and trust.
Periodic Check-In Video. Periodically send a casual and authentic video of yourself to check in so you can stay top of mind. Ideally, you can combine this with other worthy news to share (about the project, about your company, about the buyer's company/competitors, or something personal).

Technologies That Work

Backstage selling is anchored by a sales-enablement platform that covers technology for sales learning, sales content management, and sales engagement capabilities. Given the pace of change in this area, we have decided to list the latest example of how these tools can add value in a dedicated website, *www.masteringvirtualselling.com*, so we can keep this up to date as time progresses.

TAKEAWAYS

▶ Backstage selling is relatively new; and because it's so new, being good at backstage selling will give a seller a huge leg up against other sellers.

▶ Like other knowledge, being good requires consistency, practice, iteration, and constant improvement.

▶ Together, the last two chapters, covering the essence of frontstage and backstage selling should be a solid foundation for your journey toward mastering virtual selling.

▶ Backstage selling is about creating successful micro buying experiences around frontstage virtual meetings that focus on delivering a standout buyers' experience *and* "creating presence in your absence" in between meetings.

▶ Frontstage time and in-person time are precious. Focus those times on rapport building and interactive collaboration. Offload as much one-way information sharing to backstage as possible, but make sure you match backstage content to things that are most helpful to the buyers in the stage they are in.

▶ Leverage videos of yourself and independent third-party collateral to continue to build trust. Create strong micro buying experiences by bookending any frontstage virtual meetings with a pre- and post-meeting video.

▶ Continue to use templates of content, based on their effectiveness in the past.

▶ Be the first to leverage SMEs and executives like never before, using asynchronous brainstorming techniques.

▶ Because you are not on the spotlight in real time, you can do just-in-time learning yourself to support your communication and collaboration with the buyer.

▶ Know what forms of content work best. For example, short videos of one to two minutes are better than a three- to five-minute video by a mile!

▶ Leverage technologies to track what content works best at what stage so the overall buyer experience can be further optimized.

▶ Leverage technologies that record meeting calls for notetaking and for more complete follow-through.

▶ Leverage a *digital sales room* (DSR) to centralize all the interactions with the buyers in one place, over time, and deliver a superior buyer experience while providing you visibility to buyers' interest areas and levels.

ENDNOTES

1   Anna-Sophie Smith, Jakob Stöber, and Jochen Ulrich, McKinsey & Company, "How Data Analytics Helps Sales Reps Win More Deals," https://www.mckinsey.com/business-functions/marketing-and-sales/our-insights/how-data-analytics-helps-sales-reps-win-more-deals#.

2   Wikipedia, "Bing Crosby," https://en.wikipedia.org/wiki/Bing_Crosby.

3   Mary Pederson, AdAge, "Best Practices: What Is the Optimal Length for Video Content?" https://adage.com/article/digitalnext/optimal-length-video-content/299386.

4   Christina Newberry, "25 YouTube Statistics that May Surprise You: 2021 Edition," Huitesuite, https://docs.google.com/document/d/1rbiu-8Aqap4z5IfT35Q3L07ZI4FXQrnL/edit.

ENABLING VIRTUAL SELLING TEAMS

chapter 5

"None of us is as smart as all of us."
—Warren Bennis

I n the last two chapters, we discussed key elements of virtual selling across both frontstage and backstage—for individual sellers. But in order for sellers to be successful in virtual selling, the sales organization must also adapt to a new way of working. This chapter is designed to help the sales executives and management think through the changes necessary to run a successful virtual selling team.

If you are a seller and need ammunition to persuade your organization to support virtual selling, content in this chapter will help provide a proven vision on "what good looks like" for top organizations. We will summarize and distill key points we learned from interacting with hundreds of companies around a new vision of team selling and sales enablement that is critical to virtual selling success.

THERE IS A NEW WAY OF THINKING

Old selling is much more about a rep's singular ability to build rapport, solve problems, and articulate value to the buyer—mostly by him or herself. Virtual selling opens up the possibility of team selling—tapping help from SMEs and executives, leveraging just-in-time learning, and executing value-added backstage activities, which together, when executed correctly, deliver a superior buyer experience. Companies that rely too much on lone-wolf sellers will not be able to compete against pack hunting in the virtual selling world. Selling as a pack allows individuals to specialize and play to their strengths and their role in selling. A collaborative team also learns, adapts, and overcomes challenges much faster than lone wolves. A collaborative selling team will consistently outperform a team of lone wolves.

> *Lone-wolf sellers can no longer compete against pack hunting in the virtual selling world. Team selling, when done correctly, delivers a superior buyer experience.*

Organizations also need to evolve to a new way of recognizing success. The strong trend we are seeing is that successful sellers of the future are those who not only hit their individual targets but also are most helpful to their peers. Companies that recognize and reward these individuals will strengthen the entire team toward mastering virtual selling.

Companies that are successful in virtual selling must support their sellers on an ongoing basis and help them make the transition effectively. This requires helping them acquire new skills and knowledge applicable to the new frontstage and backstage selling activities that form the backbone of virtual selling. The additional specialization, coordination, and collaboration require a different team structure and processes than in-person selling.

Companies that succeed in virtual selling help their sellers acquire new skills and knowledge applicable to the new frontstage and backstage selling activities that form the backbone of virtual selling.

ENABLING VIRTUAL SELLING

So what does it look like for a company to be enabled in virtual selling? There are three main elements: people, processes, and technology.

People

For the people element, think about specialized resources that may help the team be more productive in frontstage and backstage selling. We find that top candidates from the following specializations help a sales team drastically escalate its productivity:

▶   Assistants and coordinators: Since virtual selling does not require travel and thus allows sellers to schedule many more meetings, and since sellers no longer have the luxury of popping in to see a client, every frontstage interaction needs to be scheduled. Tools can help (we have suggestions in our backstage arsenal), but nothing beats a resource dedicated to this function. In addition, this resource could help make backstage activities run smoother and error free.

▶ SMEs and executives: Determine the level of support you need from a pool of SMEs and executives and identify ways to utilize them. One very effective way is to have them participate in frontstage virtual meetings by providing helpful content (e.g., a video recording) that can be shared in frontstage or that can be sent from backstage activities. Pilot a few of these, *based on what the team collectively needs,* test and iterate a few, and your team will be hooked by the power and efficiency of either live or prerecorded content from your best resources. They will ask for more.

▶ Technology specialists: Technological help is critical. Virtual selling is much more technology dependent in many ways. Having specialists who know how to help you with troubleshooting frontstage problems and ensuring backstage technology is working is as important as having someone to make sure your laptop and phone are working. Don't rely on your individual sellers to become total technology gurus. Of course they need to know more, but it would be counterproductive to require them to fend for themselves when it comes to the complete set of technologies and tools involved.

To summarize, in the "people" element of enabling virtual selling, specialization allows you to:

▶ leverage lower cost resources (i.e., assistants and coordinators) for tasks that sellers shouldn't be doing;

▶ set up a repeatable and efficient way of engaging
  your high-cost (i.e., SMEs and executives)
  resources; and

▶ ensure sellers focus on selling, leaving tasks that
  require other specialized knowledge to the experts
  (i.e., technology specialists).

PROCESS AND TECHNOLOGY

The process and technology elements of enabling virtual
selling require an anchoring technology and repeatable
processes principle for each of the frontstage and
backstage selling arenas.

For frontstage selling, the anchoring technology is the
virtual meeting platform. The value of a reliable and
drama-free platform cannot be overstated. Without a
working platform, there is no frontstage selling.

As mentioned in the chapter on frontstage selling,
success is dependent on how various meetings are run.
In a sales organization, there should be a process in
place that constantly examines what works and what
doesn't—to help improve the templates your team
needs to orchestrate frontstage activities; this allows
sellers to become fluent in executing them. Working as
a team, they can home in on what works best for your
company in producing results, versus having each seller
create their own set of templates and learning from the
experience. Success comes faster for teams that are set up
to share best practices and disseminate and standardize
"what good looks like."

*Companies should have a process
in place that constantly examines
what works and what doesn't
so they can help improve the
templates their team needs to
orchestrate frontstage activities.*

For backstage selling, companies should have processes
in place that support micro buying experiences
(before or after a frontstage meeting) as well as
ongoing creating-presence-in-your-absence nurturing
communication to help provide beneficial services
to buyers along their buying cycle. As in frontstage
processes, it's all about repeatability and testing to find
the set that works best for your organization.

*For backstage selling, companies should
have in place processes that support
micro buying experiences (before or
after a frontstage meeting) and ongoing
creating-presence-in-your-absence
nurturing communication.*

From a technology perspective, the anchoring
technology for backstage selling is a *sales-enablement
platform*. (Learn more about this at our website:
www.masteringvirtualselling.com.) More precisely, it's a set
of capabilities within a sales-enablement platform that
specifically enables the backstage selling processes.

Sales enablement is actually a relatively new discipline that comes from the high-tech industry in which a dedicated team's sole objective is to help sellers be as effective and efficient as possible. Some of you may have never heard the term "sales enablement"; others may already have this discipline operating in your company. In either case, in order to ground everyone in the same definition, we have included a gray sidebar section that dives into the holistic picture of what a sales-enablement platform is, so we won't labor it here. As you will see in that section, virtual selling is one subset—the tip of the iceberg, if you will—of the sales-enablement function. The purpose of this book is not to teach you everything about sales enablement, but to give you content surrounding virtual selling. If you are a sales professional, this is going to be a big part of your future.

Sales Enablement Evolved eBook from Allego,
Available at *www.masteringvirtualselling.com*

However, before we go there, let's look at the features within a sales-enablement platform that are needed to support virtual selling:

▶ Allows reps to quickly share digital content (documents and videos) with individual buyers (typically via email) *and* track how the content is being used;

▶ Allows reps (with two clicks) to generate videos of themselves talking to the buyer or using a voiceover PowerPoint presentation; we discussed types of content that can be generated by this approach in chapter 4;

Example of content creation in Allego

▶ Allows reps to create *interactive* content that goes above and beyond sending a trackable document or rep-generated video. Interactive content allows the buyer to respond or collaborate with the seller backstage. Again, we gave some examples in chapter 4; however, as a refresher, here are some common examples: a video that asks the seller to select a time for the next meeting, an embedded poll that asks key questions before a meeting (or follow up after a meeting), a list of "fun facts" buyers can respond to, etc. The key here is not making the feature so complicated that sellers have to do more than a few clicks or put in extensive energy to learn how to do it themselves.

▶ Allows sellers to easily create individual digital sales rooms (DSRs) for each opportunity in their pipeline; this allows the buyer to experience a personalized, clutter-free, and efficient journey between the buyer and the seller. The DSR is where sellers share pertinent content with the buyer, store recordings of previous meetings, answer questions on demand, chat to answer questions, and allow various individuals from the same buying organization to self-serve on content that is relevant to their needs.

Allego Digital Sales Room Example

▶ Allows the system to analyze *all* intelligence
gathered from recorded calls, shared content, and
DSR activities, as well as other information from
your CRM system. It also allows the system to
leverage AI to produce *actionable intelligence* to help
make recommendations on what messaging to share,
what content to share, and even what sellers may
need to learn and improve.

Obviously, a seller cannot just "wing it" when enabling
virtual selling. In order to maximize its value in the new
normal world of selling, companies must realize how
important this discipline is. However, a key takeaway
from this chapter is that executives and sales leaders
should not be discouraged by the number of adjustments
needed to pivot toward virtual selling. Your competitors
are likely struggling with adapting to virtual selling too.
Each incremental effort you make, you will be able to
magnify that difference to selling success. But if you fall
behind in your maturity journey toward virtual selling
and sales enablement in general, don't be surprised if
one day you find your company is hopelessly behind the
competition.

*Don't be discouraged by the number
of adjustments needed to pivot
toward virtual selling because your
competitors are likely struggling with
adapting to virtual selling too!*

Supporting Sales Teams with Modern Sales Enablement

Definitions of Sales Enablement from Some of the Most Respected Analysts in This Area:

Gartner: "Sales enablement is the activity, systems, processes, and information that support and promote knowledge-based sales interactions with clients and prospects."

SiriusDecisions: "The job of sales enablement is to ensure that salespeople possess the skills, knowledge, assets, and processes to maximize every buyer interaction."

Forrester: "Sales enablement is a strategic, ongoing process that equips employees with the ability to consistently have a valuable conversation with the right set of customer stakeholders at each stage of the customer's journey."

CSO Insights: "Sales enablement is a strategic cross-functional discipline designed to increase sales results and productivity by providing integrated content, training, and coaching services."[1]

The Sales-Enablement Function

An overarching function that can mean success or failure in virtual selling is the sales-enablement function. At its core, sales enablement is the ongoing process of maximizing revenue per rep, by ensuring sellers convey the right concept using the right content throughout each stage of the buying process. Sales enablement maximizes every point of engagement salespeople have with buyers and improves the experience they provide.

A team-selling culture and dynamics are essential to success. Sales teams need the support of a sales-enablement function to be successful in navigating a more complex world of virtual selling and hybrid selling (a mixture of both in-person and virtual).

Given its powerful impact on the bottom line, next-level sales enablement is no longer optional. It's a crucial element for survival, growth, and success in today's ultra-competitive economy.

> *Next-level sales enablement is a crucial element for survival, growth, and success in today's ultracompetitive economy.*

It's Time to Evolve Your Sales-Enablement Approach

Effectively implementing sales enablement requires careful planning to rebalance resources. Will the plans and processes you put in place set you up for future success?

Today you need to take a holistic approach to meet long-term needs. An innovative sales learning and enablement strategy can help you deliver the knowledge, content, collaboration, and insights to drive results in the next normal—and you don't have to spend a fortune on multiple technology solutions to do it.

Five Essential Components of Modern Sales Enablement

These are the essential capabilities of the modern sales-enablement tech stack:

1. Onboarding and Training

The most effective sales-enablement programs bolster traditional training with reinforcement and collaboration tools that ensure what was trained is retained and what is retained turns into actions and behavior change. This is sometimes called "modern sales learning," which differentiates from the old approach of one-shot training and expecting people to remember what was said (they don't!). Sales training includes onboarding new hires and supporting them with continuous learning and reinforcement on product information, messaging, competitive positioning, and the skills needed to have valuable interactions throughout the virtual sales process.

Ensuring that what was trained is retained is an important element of an effective sales-enablement program.

2. Launches and Rollouts

Sales enablement also supports launches and rollouts. Clear communication is essential for new product launches and product line mergers. Sales managers need the ability to deliver messaging, share information consistently in a timely manner, and help reps hone their talking points. Whether for an existing product or service or a new offering, enabling managers with prerecorded practice videos so they can deliver point-in-time coaching and feedback accelerates the mastery of any new pitch.

3. **Content Management**

    Sales enablement drives the creation, distribution, and management of customer-facing sales assets and internal sales-training content. All content needs to be readily discoverable, easy to consume, trackable, and reusable across the sales organization. The sources should be a mixture of marketing or customer-facing content and just-in-time learning (YouTube-like) content, as well as time-sensitive and up-to-date internal content that continuously evolves with the changing market (e.g., competitive information, best customer stories to tell, and win-and-loss reports). We call this "agile content," and it often leverages the field to generate these types of content in a timely way, from sources they trust, and on subjects relevant to current selling situations. In addition, it's not enough to simply make content assets available; sellers must know when and how to use these resources to deliver maximum impact to their prospects. Leveraging analytics and teams that know what's working—and what's not—can improve sales content to be even more effective across different situations over time.

The creation, distribution, and management of customer-facing sales assets and internal sales-training content are driven by sales enablement. All content must be readily discoverable, easy to consume, trackable, and reusable across the sales organization.

4. Coaching and Collaboration

Sales enablement extends not only to sales reps but also to sales managers. Equipping frontline managers to inspire, motivate, and support reps with good coaching and communication skills improves seller productivity and leads to better results. You need a tech solution that supports formal and ad hoc coaching for reps and managers to hone their skills. Recorded call (game-tape) coaching capabilities with actionable AI-powered insight enables managers to provide the most effective point-in-time feedback.

You can get the best results by equipping frontline managers to inspire, motivate, and support reps with good coaching and communication skills.

Sales enablement facilitates communication within the team and across other functions. In particular, alignment and continuous collaboration with the marketing team is essential. Without it, reps miss out on the insights marketing is gathering from its top-of-funnel campaigns, and marketing misses the chance to shape its campaigns based on firsthand sales conversations. Technology that helps your team empower reps with information from all departments is crucial.

Without alignment and continuous collaboration with the marketing team, reps miss out on the insights marketing is gathering from its top-of-funnel campaigns, and marketing misses the chance to shape its campaigns based on firsthand sales conversations.

5. Virtual Selling

The final element of modern sales enablement is virtual selling. As we have described throughout this book, successful virtual selling depends on learning new skills and tactics, implementing a frontstage and backstage strategy, and implementing a technology solution that allows sellers to nurture prospects, share information, conduct demos, and host meetings without the benefit of sitting side by side with a prospect. Frontstage virtual selling technology is anchored on a drama-free virtual meeting platform. Backstage virtual selling capabilities include the ability for sellers to create and share ad hoc videos, track and analyze content to optimize success, transcribe and analyze meeting recordings for note-taking and seller skill improvement, and create digital sales rooms to improve seller-buyer collaboration.

Successful virtual selling depends on learning new skills and tactics, implementing a frontstage and backstage strategy, and implementing a technology solution that allows sellers to nurture prospects, share information, conduct demos, and host meetings without the benefit of sitting side by side with a prospect.

Sales teams that adopt a modern sales-enablement strategy that encompasses these five components can accelerate the sales cycle, drive higher average contract values, and boost profitability in the sales organization.

Virtual Selling Technology

There is a set of key technologies that sellers must master to be successful. As we discussed in chapters 3 and 4, a video conference platform is critical for frontstage activities. And capabilities that allow a seller to share content and collaborate *asynchronously* are critical for backstage activities (e.g., recording calls and automated note-taking, digital sales rooms, and trackable shared content).

These technologies can be summarized into four types: learning, content, coaching, and collaboration. While some organizations choose siloed solutions for each capability, there's a new breed of integrated software platforms that offers a holistic approach to sales enablement. These solutions enable all five of the components of sales enablement described above.

Here's a quick overview of the four types of technology that you, as a sales manager, want to make sure you're taking advantage of to enable virtual selling.

▶ Modern learning technology: Managers need a way to onboard, train, and develop sellers at all stages of their careers with technology that delivers information at the moment of need. Modern learning technology allows managers to deliver formal courses, reinforcement learning, coaching, and just-in-time learning that ensure what's learned is retained and applied, resulting in true behavior change.

▶ Content-management technology: The key to virtual seller efficiency is access to key content. This requires an effective content-management platform. Content management does much more than simply house sales collateral. It's a place that allows a seller to access *all* the content they need at the moment of need. This means: (a) reference material, YouTube-like video, how-tos," etc., (b) marketing collateral, and (c) "agile content" (short shelf-life, time-sensitive content relevant to sellers, often generated by the field, from trusted sources).

▶ Coaching technology: Coaching starts with knowing where and when sellers need improvement. This can be as simple as focusing on new hires or low performers or focusing on training everyone on a brand-new launch (i.e., new material that needs to be put into practice). Or coaching can be more advanced, such as analyzing which part of a deal cycle a particular seller is having the most difficulty with (most sellers are strong in just parts of a buying/selling cycle) and focusing coaching attention there. There are several types of coaching that are essential: (1) self-coaching based on indicator or weaknesses identified, (2) one-to-one managerial (or AI) coaches or dedicated trainers to provide feedback, and (3) "coaching at scale"—where there are technology and processes to systematically identify which seller and which part (even down to which meeting recorded!) should be focused on to provide the all-important feedback to help a seller overcome challenges. There are technologies that help do this automatically and asynchronously—to help sales managers/trainers focus their limited bandwidth on the most important moment-of-need coaching.

**COACHING ON
VIDEO PRACTICE OR CALLS**

▶ Collaboration technology: Now that we have seen the power of asynchronous collaboration that can take place between a buyer and a seller in backstage, free from the limitations of time and place, we can see how this asynchronous collaboration can also help teams collaborate internally more effectively. The modern sales-enablement platform not only serves as the backbone for backstage selling; it also facilitates asynchronous team collaboration. For example, a seller desperately needs feedback on an important presentation in two days. There is no chance this seller will be able to book a meeting among the seven people who need to brainstorm. In the old days, the seller would go to his/her manager or try to talk to an SME to see if either one could solve the problem. Armed with a modern sales-enablement platform, this rep can record a voiceover PowerPoint presentation, send it out to all seven SMEs, and get their feedback (asynchronously)—all without having to schedule a meeting on the calendar.

Sales managers should make sure they're taking advantage of these four types of technology to enable virtual selling: modern learning, content management, coaching, and collaboration.

Sales enablement has arrived. If you support a sales force—as a sales manager, sales trainer, content or product marketer, or sales enablement pro—this is your moment.

That's because it's more important than ever for companies to equip their sales teams to produce at the highest levels. With the uncertain economy, safety restrictions due to the pandemic, and tightening budgets, making quota is tougher—and more critical—than ever.

Sales enablement—when done well—is proven to drive results. High-performing sales companies are twice as likely to provide ongoing training as low-performing ones[2]. And the use of sales-enablement solutions has grown by 567 percent over the last three years.[3]

High-performing sales companies
are twice as likely to provide ongoing
training as low-performing ones.

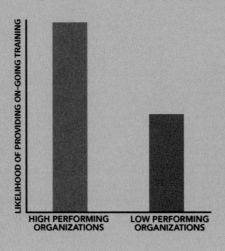

Altogether, beyond the technologies needed to enable frontstage and backstage selling, establishing and executing on all these key sales-enablement processes will be pivotal to virtual-selling success. But all these need to be backed by a willing team. Team selling beats lone wolves. Declare a higher standard—one that says hitting quota is no longer a hallmark of a top seller. The seller must do that *and* be a valuable resource to other sellers. We know companies that offer incentives and recognition of their most skilled team members/SMEs to encourage cultural change. Create a learning culture to deal with expected and constant change that is coming. (In a 2016 *New York Times* article that featured Yuchun entitled "The Value of a Daily Mistake," he was asked, "How do you hire?" His response was, "I look for people who are not set in their ways, and who are interested in learning and growing. You can tell that just by whether their eyes sparkle when they talk about the most rewarding experience in their life.[4])

Remember, learning has nothing to do with sitting in a classroom (or online) and listening to a one-way lecture. Create new roles in the sales organization and draft resources from marketing and operations to help with agile content creation and coordination of resources (SMEs, execs, and technical resources) to deliver a repeatable and exceptional buyer experience across the entire team.

Virtual selling is part of a larger capability; if you want to know more, go to ***masteringvirtualselling.com***.

TAKEAWAYS

▶ Lone-wolf sellers can no longer compete against pack hunting in the virtual-selling world. Team selling, when done correctly, delivers a superior buyer experience.

▶ Enabling virtual selling involves three main elements: people, processes, and technologies.

▷ People: Leveraging executives, SMEs, and coordinators, helps a sales team drastically escalate its productivity.

▷ Technology:

☐ The key technology for frontstage selling is the virtual-meeting platform. It must be reliable and drama free.

☐ The key technology for backstage selling is a *sales-enablement platform,* which enables reps to quickly share digital content, generate videos of themselves or voiceover PowerPoint presentations to communicate with the buyer, create interactive content, and create DSRs. It also allows the system to analyze intelligence gathered from multiple sources of information and leverage AI to produce *actionable intelligence* to help make recommendations on what messaging and content to share, and even what sellers may need to learn and improve.

▷ Processes: Companies should have processes in place that constantly examine what works and what doesn't to allow sellers to become fluent in executing frontstage activities as well as backstage activities that support micro buying experiences and ongoing creating–presence–in–your–absence communication.

▶ Executives and sales leaders, listen up! Since your competitors are likely struggling with adapting to virtual selling as well, you should not be discouraged by the number of adjustments needed to pivot toward virtual selling. However, falling behind in your maturity journey toward virtual selling and sales enablement in general could put you hopelessly behind the competition.

▶ An overall sales-enablement program is the ongoing process of maximizing revenue per rep, by ensuring sellers convey the right concept using the right content throughout each stage of the buying process. Next-level sales enablement is a crucial element for survival, growth, and success in today's ultracompetitive economy.

▶ There are five essential components of modern sales enablement that can accelerate the sales cycle, drive higher average contract values, and boost profitability in the sales organization:

  ▷ onboarding and training;

  ▷ launches and rollouts;

  ▷ content management;

  ▷ coaching and collaboration; and

  ▷ virtual selling.

▶ Sellers must master these types of key technologies to be successful:

▷ modern learning technology;

▷ content-management technology;

▷ coaching technology; and

▷ collaboration technology.

▶ It's more important than ever for companies to equip their sales teams to produce at the highest levels. Establishing and executing on all these key sales-enablement processes will be pivotal to virtual-selling success. But all these need to be backed by a willing team. Companies must create a learning culture to deal with expected and constant change that is coming.

ENDNOTES

1 "Gartner Glossary, https://www.gartner.com/en/information-technology/glossary/sales-enablement, "What is Sales Enablement, https://go.forrester.com/blogs/what-is-sales-enablement/, and CSO Insights, Fifth Annual Sales Enablement Study, https://salesenablement.pro/assets/2019/10/CSO-Insights-5th-Annual-Sales-Enablement-Study.pdf.

2 Aja Frost, "60 Key Sales Statistics That'll Help You Sell Smarter in 2021," HubSpot, https://blog.hubspot.com/sales/sales-statistics.

3 "2019 SaleTech Benchmark Survey," file:///C:/Users/nonie/Downloads/SST_2019_SalesTech_Benchmark_Survey-c.p.

4 Adam Bryant, "Yuchun Lee of Allego: The Value of a Daily Mistake," New York Times, https://www.nytimes.com/2016/12/16/business/yuchun-lee-of-allego-the-value-of-a-daily-mistake.html).

STEPPING CONFIDENTLY INTO THE FUTURE

chapter 6

*"Success at work is fundamental
to human happiness."*
—Yuchun Lee, Allego CEO

By using the framework we've established in this book, studying it in earnest, and executing on what we've shared, you should be well on your way to becoming a master virtual seller. You have learned that the world today requires mastering the art of orchestration for success. A maestro creates beautiful music by integrating everything together to create the desired experience for the audience. If you want to succeed in this world, you too must learn to orchestrate the pieces that together will produce the results you want.

*When you master the art of
orchestration, as the maestro you can
bring everything together to create the
desired experience for the audience.*

Mastering virtual selling requires that you integrate both the frontstage and backstage to create an effective micro buying experience and presence in your absence, making you a trusted advisor to the buyers and helping you achieve your desired outcome.

So what's next? Well, you have the knowledge of how to master virtual selling, but you are not yet a master. To get there from here takes a dedication to deliberate practice and continued learning.

For example, a beginner may be able to read sheet music and know what the notes are. Yet when he/she plays a piece of music, it will sound totally different than when a master pianist plays it because it's the master's consummate timing and cadence and style that makes it beautiful. In the same way, you may have to first endure and even embrace an awkwardness in your attempts at virtual selling. However, in the end, with repetition, practice, and intestinal fortitude, you can push through and become a master.

A FINAL WORD ON MASTERY

According to yourdictionary.com, there are sixty-four different definitions of mastery. The definition that has informed our thinking in this book is "a person very skilled and able in some work, profession, science, etc.; expert."

For the purposes of this book, mastery is defined as "a person very skilled and able in some work, profession, science, etc.; expert."

When you think about what masters have in common, whether it's great athletes, such as the golf master Jack Nicklaus or quarterback Tom Brady, great artists from da Vinci to Picasso, or masters featured in this book, such as Erica Feidner and Ben Zander, they've all developed their mastery by doing something they loved over a long period of time. In addition, they all began as apprentices in one form or another.

In the movie *Keep On Keepin' On,* we see one of the most powerful examples of how an apprentice becomes a master. It tells the story of how legendary jazz musician Clark Terry, at age ninety-three, based on his journey to mastery, becomes the mentor of a twenty-three-year-old pianist named Justin Kauflin, who suffered from crippling stage fright.

In the movie, Herbie Hancock says about Clark Terry, "When you hear Clark play, you hear his life. Only a master can do that, and Clark is a master."

> *"When you hear Clark play, you hear his life. Only a master can do that, and Clark is a master."*
> —Herbie Hancock

Clark Terry was also a teacher and mentor to Quincy Jones (the renowned American musician and Grammy-winning record producer). This demonstrates not only how much masters can give their apprentices on their journey, but also how gratifying it is for masters to enjoy the success of their apprentices as they develop.

The big idea is that there is joy in learning how to do something new. It's a natural state of being for children that we often forget as adults. Children don't want it to be easy; they want to keep doing it until they've mastered it. Whether it's learning to walk, swim, or ride a bike, children intuitively understand that you need to keep practicing until you have mastered the task. Capturing some of this childlike curiosity and wonder is one of the secrets to becoming a master, for it's the doing of it again and again that makes mastery a reality.

Children remind us that there is joy in learning how to do something new.

But there is more to the story. As it turns out, the quality of your teacher matters as well. As you move from apprenticeship to mastery, who you choose as your maestro makes a difference. Whether it is a peer, manager, or subject-matter experts, choosing the right master is important.

Malcolm Gladwell in his book *Outliers* says it takes 10,000 hours to master something. Whether that is precisely accurate is not the point. The point is that, in general, it takes a long time. It requires a willingness to practice even when you don't feel like it, and perhaps most importantly, especially when you don't feel like it.

Finally, since Allego is at the forefront of what is changing in the virtual-selling world, maintaining a relationship with us through our website at *www. masteringvirtualselling.com* and other parts of our community will give you a leg up on understanding those changes and the chance to interact with other masters.

Let's end with the same question we asked at the beginning: There are three types of people in this world—those who make things happen, those who watch them happen, and those who wonder what happened. **Which kind will you be?**

TAKEAWAYS

▶ If you want to succeed in today's world, you must master the art of orchestration; learn to orchestrate the pieces that together will produce the results you want.

▶ Mastering virtual selling requires that you integrate both the frontstage and backstage areas of selling in order to create presence in your absence, making you a trusted advisor to the buyers and helping you achieve your desired outcome.

▶ The definition of master that has informed our thinking in this book is "a person very skilled and able in some work, profession, science, etc.; expert."

▶ When you think about what masters have in common, they've all developed their mastery by doing something they loved over a long period of time. In addition, they all began as apprentices in one form or another.

▶ Clark Terry exemplifies both mastery and being a mentor.

▶ We can learn from children that there's joy in learning something new. Capturing a childlike curiosity and wonder is one of the secrets to becoming a master, understanding that it's the repetition of doing it over and over again that makes mastery a reality.

▶ As you move from apprenticeship to mastery, who you choose as your maestro makes a difference. Whether it is a peer, manager, or subject-matter experts, choosing the right master is important.

GLOSSARY

ad hoc, 83: Created or done for a particular purpose as necessary

arsenal, xix: An array of resources available for a certain purpose

asynchronous, xix: Communication that is not simultaneous or time bound

backstage selling, xviii: Collaboration with a buyer digitally in an asynchronous way (i.e., with no requirement for both parties to be locked into a specific time to do so). This may involve sending the buyer an email or video or something else such as a picture, a link to your website, or a discount that they may consume and respond to later, at a time of their choosing.

breathing space, 58: An opportunity to direct the attention of the audience away from the presenter in order to involve the audience more through a change of pace and to give the presenter a moment to collect his or her thoughts. Examples include showing a video, directing someone else to comment, or having audience members write something down—so their eyes come off the presenter for a few seconds or a few minutes.

collaboration, xvii: The action of working with someone to produce or create something

creating presence in your absence, 119: Includes a series of communications and activities that help keep you top of mind with the buyer. This can include relevant collateral, SME content/videos, and third-party information useful to the buyer in the sales process.

digital sales room (DSR), 116: A "digital place" that is like a dedicated website on steroids—one that is created *just* for this one buyer for this one buying journey with you. It may include a personal welcome video from you to "meet them at the door" and welcome your buyer, a list of relevant research or testimonials relevant to the buyer, threaded chat and discussions to help answer questions, and recordings of previous meetings so everyone is on the same page.

frontstage selling, xviii: Synchronous collaboration with the participants, where you have live *virtual* interactions with each other through a Zoom meeting, a phone call, etc., versus in person.

master, xv: A person very skilled and able in some work, profession, science, etc; expert.

meeting kits, 49: Custom-built packages that contain tailored items you will be referring to during the meetings

maestro, xv: A distinguished musician or a great or distinguished figure in any sphere

micro buying experience, 32: A specific, collaborative virtual meeting that is preceded and followed by communications between the seller and the buyer. The typical pattern is a communication before the frontstage meeting designed to set the stage and usually includes an agenda and LinkedIn profile information on each participant to save attendees' time. Following the frontstage meeting, it includes a summarization of key points and next steps. This process is repeated throughout a sales process until the buyer's journey is complete.

one-third rule, 45: Whatever you would do in an in-person meeting, do only one-third of it during a virtual sales meeting.

rapport, 6: A relationship characterized by agreement, mutual understanding, or empathy that makes communication possible or easy.

sales enablement, xvii: sales enablement is a strategic approach to supporting sellers with the skills, information, processes, and technology they need to be as productive as possible by providing holistic onboarding and training, product and message launch, content management, coaching and collaboration, and virtual and in-person selling.

Sherpa guide, 116: A member of the Himalayan people renowned for their skill in mountaineering; someone who acts as a guide for you

synchronous, xix: Communication that happens in real time

SME, 58: Subject-matter expert

targeted polling, 122: Calling on specific members of the audience and asking them to share their feedback with the rest of the group, giving the presenter the ability to tailor the remaining portion of the presentation to more successfully influence the audience

virtual–meeting platform, 48: Virtual-meeting platforms are video applications and software that bring people together over the Internet. Usually, this software includes a form of video conferencing, as well as tools like chat, reactions, and screen sharing. Examples of this software include Zoom, Webex, Google Meet, GotoMeeting, and Teams

virtual selling, xiii: Working a deal remotely when the seller and the buyer can't meet in person

ACKNOWLEDGMENTS

"Never doubt that a small group of committed people can change the world, indeed it's the only thing that ever has."
—Margaret Mead

I t's easy to take for granted the incredible technology that facilitated this virtual book collaboration with so many people. We have been consistently impressed by the Zoom platform that we used during the writing of this book and still marvel that with one click we could connect to the team members who were located in various parts of the United States.

We want to thank the many people—clients, partners, friends, and family—who have supported us in the writing of this book.

A partial list includes:

The Allego Team:

▶ Wayne St. Amand

▶ Ginna Hall

▶ Louis Abate

▶ Annie Taber

▶ Jennifer Demerle

The Tony Jeary International Team:

▶ Eloise Worden

▶ Nonie Jobe

▶ Ella Imrie

▶ Daniel Marold

▶ Tawnya Austin

Special thanks to:

▶ Paul B. Brown, for demonstrating your mastery that helped us bring this book to life

▶ Dan Sullivan, for providing Mark with the initial concept for the frontstage/backstage model that evolved into content for this book. Dan remains an example of how a great teacher can inspire an apprentice towards mastery.

▶ Ben Zander, for demonstrating the power of possibility thinking and living his life in a way that inspires on the journey toward mastery everywhere

▶ Erika Feidner, for demonstrating what good selling looks like and proving the importance of passion and knowledge to differentiate a sales person to become a trusted resource

And a special thanks to our wives, Agustina Lee, Sheri Magnacca, and Tammy Jeary, who helped make space for our collaboration—despite a pandemic—whether our meetings were early in the morning, late at night, or whenever else we needed time to collaborate over the course of the writing process, allowing us to complete this book. Thank you!

APPENDIX
Book Summary for

INTRODUCTION

▶ Virtual selling is about working a deal
remotely when you can't be there in person.
It is not just a series of Zoom meetings!
In order to be successful, you must use all
the tools in your arsenal to understand a
prospect's mindset in a virtual setting.

Why Read This Book?

▶ This book will help improve results for executives, sales leaders, and individual sellers. We are all now apprentices in this new world of virtual selling.

Becoming a Master (or More Specifically, a Maestro)

▶ The cover reveals the essence of the book—learning to be a maestro at orchestrating the moving parts in the buying process. Ben Zander, founder and director of the Boston Philharmonic Orchestra, is an extraordinary example of a maestro who masterfully orchestrates the frontstage and backstage activities to achieve the desired results. The same concept applies to mastering virtual selling.

The Payoff

▶ You will understand how to master virtual selling and stay ahead of the competition, as well as discovering new skills and techniques to help you be more productive while traveling less.

Who We Are

▶ Yuchun Lee, CEO and co-founder of Allego, has a proven business track record, serving as CEO of marketing automation provider Unica, guiding it through a successful IPO and sale to IBM. Yuchun is also an executive in residence at venture firm General Catalyst Partners, the executive chairman of customer experience software firm Clarabridge, serves on the board of Vertex Pharmaceuticals (NASDAQ: VRTX), and is an executive advisor with Summit Partners, a global venture and private equity firm.

▶ Mark Magnacca, president and co-founder of Allego, has an extensive background and track record of bringing ideas and businesses to life. After starting a financial planning company right out of college and selling it a decade later, he then started a sales consulting business to support a wide range of financial services companies as they began their digital transformation. This work led to the founding of Allego. He's the author of *So What? How to Communicate What Really Matters to Your Audience* and *The Product is YOU!*

▶ Tony Jeary, strategist, executive coach, and facilitator, is known as The RESULTS Guy™ because he helps clients get the right results faster. He is a unique powerful facilitator and subject-matter expert who has influenced millions worldwide, including personally coaching dozens of CEOs from the Fortune 500 and the Forbes Richest 400. He has authored over 60 books, 26 on the subject of presentation effectiveness.

▶ Our goal is to get everyone everywhere to rethink how they sell.

Our Promise to You

▶ This book will transform your approach to virtual selling and provide you with epiphanies to enhance your journey all the way to mastery.

What's Ahead

▶ Chapter 1: The difference between the selling and buying cycle, what comprises *good* selling, and three tools to get you there.

▶ Chapter 2: Tools and frameworks that will allow you to create a consistently compelling buying experience.

▶ Chapters 3 and 4: Key differences between frontstage and backstage and tools to build and highlight the strengths of each.

▶ Chapter 5: Enabling virtual-selling teams to optimize your results and frameworks for sales enablement.

▶ Chapter 6: Tying together all of the factors discussed, ensuring that you succeed in the new virtual-selling world.

If You Are Skeptical: A Case Study

CHAPTER 1:
CREATING AN EXCEPTIONAL
BUYING EXPERIENCE

▶ Mastering virtual selling starts with mastering the art of selling. You will not succeed in virtual selling if you are not good at selling—period.

▶ Al Pacino was a stage actor before being a movie actor. After excelling in the live format of acting, he went on to become a master in the virtual format.

▶ If you are new to selling, now is a great time to build the right habits to help you succeed.

What Good Selling Is

▶ Good selling is grounded in an exceptional buying experience. Sellers tend to focus on the selling cycle versus the buying cycle. Today's buyers don't want to be sold; they want to buy. They are concerned about their needs—not your process. To be successful, think of selling as a service to the buyer and fuse the two cycles together as two sides of the same coin.

► An appropriate buying/selling cycle includes:
  ▷ researching and building rapport;
  ▷ understanding and solving buyer problems;
  ▷ leveraging success.

STEP ONE: Researching and Building Rapport

► The more research you do, the more impressed your buyer will be. Curiosity is one of the most valuable traits a person in sales can have. Today there is so much information available, and it's free. Da Vinci would thrive in this era, as he was intensely curious and gained inspiration from many angles. Curiosity fueled his research and enabled him to become a *master* in every sense of the word.

► There is no substitute for research. At a minimum, you should research your buyer's LinkedIn profile, Google your contact and his/her organization, and study the organization's website. Masters will use the info on LinkedIn to search for common connections and seek out personal, firsthand information.

Emotions Matter

► People buy based on emotion, not logic. Ensure you connect with a prospect by bringing your unique vibe to the meeting.

▶ Most importantly, building rapport is based on trust. Send credible info before the meeting, be dependable, honor commitments, and be authentic in order to build rapport. Genuine interest builds trust, which is built over time.

STEP TWO: Understanding and Solving Your Customer's Problems

▶ The ability to understand the buyer's problem is fundamental to mastery.

▶ Listening is a key part of understanding the buyer's problem. People want to be heard, and that requires listening well. What sets masters apart is their ability to let the other person talk as well as their skill in guiding the conversation by asking thoughtful, relevant questions. Be willing to get comfortable with silence.

▶ When Multiple People Need to Say Yes

▷ You often have multiple stakeholders in a selling situation, and understanding the needs of each stakeholder is important. Different people also have varying levels of influence in awarding you the business.

▷ Sellers need the most current information— including market conditions, customer insights, and competitive intelligence, and even relevant win/loss stories—in order to provide insight and help buyers make decisions.

▷ It isn't enough to understand the current market environment. You have to be able to solve your customer's problems in order to close the deal.

> To be a problem solver, you need to be able to remove obstacles for the buyer.

STEP THREE: Leveraging Success

▶ Master sellers don't end their engagement after the signature; they protect their reputation by making sure they deliver value to their customers. The worst thing a seller can do is to move on after the sale is completed.

▶ Get feedback on how you can improve.

▶ Follow through on both the sale and the relationship, leading to an increased chance of a referral.

▶ The three Rs—repurchase, referral, and reference—are an essential concept in leveraging success.

The Takeaway from This Chapter:

▶ Mastering virtual selling starts with the basics—you cannot be a master at *virtual* selling without first mastering the art of selling.

CHAPTER 2:
THE POWER OF ORCHESTRATION

▶ Maestro Benjamin Zander's performances are spellbinding, both because of his delivery and his engagement with the audience, as he brings energy, enthusiasm, and caring to every interaction.

A New Kind of Music

▶ Think of selling as a musical event. You, as the conductor, bring emotion and the rhythm that can be transformative, just like music.

▶ There are many things in the virtual and in-person selling world that remain the same—or at least mostly the same. However, there is an expanded opportunity in the world of virtual selling that requires a big shift in mindset.

Lessons from the Master—or Maestro

▶ Through serendipitous circumstances, Mark got a personal invitation from Ben Zander to attend an event where he was speaking. As a result, Mark was able to observe the maestro at work in a micro buying experience cycle (backstage activities that supported the frontstage event, the ensuing frontstage event, and additional backstage activities that further complemented and enhanced the frontstage event).

▶ In the world of the performing arts, people typically fill roles in either the frontstage or backstage areas, which are both orchestrated by the maestro or the musical director to create an exceptional experience for the audience.

▶ The frontstage in an orchestra encompasses everything in front of the curtain that is real time, which includes the musicians and what they are playing in front of an audience. The backstage is everything that supports the frontstage, including rehearsal, music selection, lighting, preparation before the event, and follow-up after the concert.

The Maestro Is You

▶ The maestro—or conductor—is you, the salesperson. A maestro helps the orchestra play to its fullest potential

and ensures everything works togeth
desired experience for the audience.
for your buyers and members of your

Deliver an Exceptional Buying Experience

▶ Just as you had to learn certain skills to operate
successfully in an in-person business meeting, you
will need to learn a host of new skills that will add
value to your buyers from your virtual frontstage
and backstage arenas.

Virtual-Selling Myths

1. **Virtual selling is a *temporary* solution.**
   People around the world have proven to themselves
   that virtual meetings are a better way to interact in
   the buying and selling process for many products
   and services.

2. **Virtual selling is inferior to face-to-face selling.**
   Virtual selling allows a richer set of participants,
   both buyers and sellers, since physical place and time
   (across both the frontstage and backstage areas) are
   no longer a limitation to collaboration.

3. **Virtual selling doesn't require new skills**
   Being a good seller does not automatically make
   you good at virtual selling. Effective virtual selling
   depends on learning a full range of technologies,
   including mobile, peer-to-peer networking, and live
   and recorded video.

4. **It's hard to build rapport virtually.**
   On the surface, it's challenging to connect and
   build trust with people when you can't be with

them in person. But we believe this is *only* true at the beginning of the relationship *or* if the seller makes no attempt to modify the way they are engaging with the buyer.

5. **Buyers are not ready for virtual selling.**
The truth is, even though many sellers are eager to go back to meeting buyers face to face, most buyers are not as inclined to meet sellers in person post-pandemic. What they do want is to save time and to find solutions to their problems, and they want experts to help them make the right decisions.

The Takeaway from This Chapter:

▶ You, the salesperson, are the maestro—or conductor. Just as a maestro helps the orchestra play to its fullest potential and ensures everything works together—frontstage and backstage—to create the desired experience for the audience, you do the same for your buyers and members of your sales team.

CHAPTER 3: FRONTSTAGE SELLING

▶ Both frontstage and backstage must work seamlessly together to create an exceptional experience for the customer.

▶ We define frontstage as a *synchronous* communication and collaboration where you and the participants have live *virtual* interaction with each other through a Zoom meeting, a phone call, Facetime, or in person.

Frontstage Challenges and Opportunities

▶ Challenges:

▷ Building rapport. In virtual selling, it is harder initially to establish human-to-human connections than with in-person meetings.

▷ Reading people. It's harder to read people through a headshot on a monitor, which makes it more difficult to pick up on nuances such as body language.

▷ Keeping people's attention. You're often blind to what people are doing at the moment.

▶ Opportunities:

▷ Time. Because there is no travel or commute time involved, you can do five to ten times more virtual meetings, once you become proficient at them, than you can in-person meetings.

▷ Efficiency. You can leverage certain components that are unique to virtual selling, such as all the elements of a frontstage arsenal.

▷ Opportunity. You're all now on a level playing field that is different, even somewhat difficult, for everyone—including your competitors—so it's easier to get ahead, even without experience.

Key Elements for Tackling Frontstage Selling

1. **Make every minute count.** In order to keep your audience's attention, one of the most important elements of executing frontstage selling is *making every minute count.* You can do that by rethinking

your agenda, becoming fluent at running a virtual meeting, and scheduling meetings at twenty-five or fifty-five minute increments (versus thirty- or sixty-minute meetings) so you have a transition time to prepare and be efficient for your next call.

2. **Find new ways to build trust and rapport.** You can do this by using virtual meetings versus a phone call; building in getting-to-know-you time; finding commonality; customizing your own background; sending food, drinks, and meeting kits; using discovery questions and appropriate humor; and understanding you can make a difference.

3. **Know what content works best for collaboration.** In today's new world, all your content should still be grounded in adding value to the buying process, but it must be different in order to be effective. There are some types of content we found that work better, like content that aids in collaboration and multimedia content. Get additional support from executives and SMEs.

4. **Make effective use of technology and tools.** In virtual selling, you are totally dependent on technology, so you want to make sure you use it to its fullest extent. Use a direct connection, get the best tech, be an expert on your tools, be fluent in other meeting technology, leverage meeting recordings, and have a backup strategy.

5. **Understand perception is reality.** Review past videos; ask for feedback; and be aware of your appearance, where your eyes look on the screen, background noises, and your body language.

6. **Manage time and energy.** Keep a good command of the time, offload content if necessary, schedule breaks for long meetings, use interactive agendas, use the roll call productively, poll your participants, follow the one-third rule, and be aware of the amount of time you are speaking in proportion to others.

The Takeaway from This Chapter:

▶ Becoming a master virtual seller requires that you execute well the six key elements of frontstage selling.

CHAPTER 4:
BACKSTAGE SELLING

▶ We define backstage as any communications or collaboration that is asynchronous or is *not* happening live or in real time. Examples of this include a text message, email, video, voice mail, or a deal room.

Backstage Challenges and Opportunities:

▶ Challenges:

▷ Backstage activities are those you may need to do before the virtual meeting and often in a different—and sometimes more limited—form factor than they had been in frontstage.

▷ Backstage activities are accomplished without engaging directly with the buyer, and there's a natural delay involved when you communicate indirectly (by text, email, snail mail, voice mail, etc.) and wait for a response.

▷ Like spamming your buyers with emails, you can overdo it with backstage activities, especially if there are technologies to help make those activities as easy as pressing a few buttons.

▶ Opportunities:

▷ Research shows that buyers are more receptive to a robust backstage engagement than before, as they would rather receive information, add their own research, and digest it all at their own pace.

▷ Whatever content you create in the backstage can be more polished because you are not doing it during live interaction. And the quality will be higher since you can incorporate editing.

▷ Since you have more limited frontstage time with your buyers, backstage is a way for you to continue to be top of mind with your buyers before, after, and in between frontstage meetings. In essence, backstage activities help you create presence in your absence along the entire buying cycle.

▷ Thanks to technology in recent years, there is a whole arsenal of things you can do backstage that previously required sophisticated production to make them happen. That same technology also gives you insights that will help you analyze the situation and understand the interest level and interest areas of your buyers like never before.

▷ Unlike a virtual meeting in frontstage, where you have to perform in real time and do almost everything yourself, in backstage you can tap into your teammates and other company resources for help.

Bing Crosby: Early Video Pioneer

▶ Most people don't know that Bing Crosby played a crucial role in bringing about new technology that evolved into much of what we talk about in this book.

▷ He was an early adopter of the condenser microphone—which allowed him to sing in his informal, easygoing, and casual way.

▷ Crosby was the first major performer to prerecord his radio shows, which allowed him to control performing conditions and times, ad-lib, and edit out mistakes. Both NBC and the sponsors were adamantly opposed to prerecording, arguing that the public would not stand for canned radio broadcasts. Crosby used his clout to move the innovation forward.

▷ His company, Bing Crosby Enterprises, helped finance the development of video tape and showed the world the first video tape recording on November 11, 1951. The strategies we are recommending for using prerecorded content have been building ever since Crosby first introduced video tapes.

Goals of Backstage Selling

1. **Create a Winning Experience for Your Buyers.** Understanding what buying stage your buyer is in is critical for all backstage activities. You must get into your buyer's head so you can support them, across both frontstage and backstage, in whatever buying stage they are in.

2. **Earn Trust and Build Your Buyer's Confidence.**
   Your overall goal is to instill confidence in your
   buyers that you are the right partner for them.

Strategy of Backstage Selling

1. **Create Successful Micro Buying Experiences.** The
   buyer's journey is made up of a series of micro buying
   experiences, which is the cycle of actual collaboration
   that is taking place at any given time. Backstage selling
   helps generate highly effective experiences around
   virtual (or in-person!) meetings by pre-engaging the
   audience before the meeting *and* post-engaging the
   attendees after the meeting. In between meetings, you
   will have an opportunity to do some backstage selling
   and create presence in your absence by sharing useful
   information to the buyers, which helps you stay top of
   mind and builds your personal brand with the buyer.

   **Use Templates to Create Strong Pre/Post
   Meeting Engagements.**
   Each of these meeting types should be supported
   by backstage content, before and after the meeting.
   The best way to make this work is to have different
   templates to help you identify what needs to be
   created for the different types of meetings.

2. **Create Presence in Your Absence.** In between
   the micro buying experiences, you will have an
   opportunity to do some backstage selling and create
   presence in your absence by sharing useful information
   to the buyers. This is the process of coordinating
   backstage activities that help nurture the buying process
   favorably forward. This content can be used over and
   over again by you and your peers on your sales team.

Key Elements for Tackling Backstage Selling

1. **Focus on Content That's Both Effective and Easy.** Think about dripping information over time to choreograph the reveal of coveted information. This will not only make each content item easier to consume, but it will also increase the frequency of interactions, which builds rapport and trust.

2. **The Difference is You!** Leverage the resources you have in the backstage arena to maximize the outcome. Since you have more time to react backstage, you can beef up what you need to know with just-in-time learning (versus having to remember everything while you are in front of the buyer).

3. **Leverage Technology.** Backstage selling is also grounded in an important set of technologies.

   a. Ability to send relevant and *trackable* content via email;

   b. Ability to generate *trackable* personalized videos;

   c. Ability to generate highly effective presentations;

   d. Ability to generate content that allows buyers to interact with you;

   e. Ability to automatically take notes in frontstage virtual meetings so you can review them backstage;

   f. Ability to *centralize* the exchange of content and collaboration in an easy-to-find place digitally.

Case Study No. 2: A Micro Buying Experience

The Takeaway from This Chapter:

▶ Becoming a master virtual seller requires that you understand the goals and strategy of backstage selling, as well as the three key elements of backstage selling.

CHAPTER 5:
ENABLING VIRTUAL SELLING TEAMS

There is a New Way of Thinking

▶ Virtual selling opens up the possibility of team selling—tapping help from SMEs and executives, leveraging just-in-time learning, and executing value-added backstage activities, which together, when executed correctly, deliver a superior buyer experience.

▶ Companies that rely too much on lone-wolf sellers will not be able to compete against pack hunting in the virtual-selling world. Selling as a pack allows individuals to specialize and play to their strengths and their role in selling.

▶ Organizations that are successful in virtual selling must support their sellers on an ongoing basis and help them make the transition effectively.

Enabling Virtual Selling

▶ There are three main elements of enabling virtual selling: people, processes, and technology.

　▷ Specialization allows you to:

　　☐ leverage lower cost resources (i.e., assistants and coordinators) for tasks that sellers shouldn't be doing

　　☐ set up a repeatable and efficient way of engaging your high-cost (i.e., SMEs and executives) resources

- ☐ ensure sellers focus on selling, leaving tasks that require other specialized knowledge to the experts (i.e., technology specialists)

▷ For frontstage selling, the anchoring technology is the virtual-meeting platform.

▷ For backstage selling, organizations should have processes and technology in place, by using a sales-enablement platform such as Allego that supports micro buying experiences (typically before or after a frontstage meeting) as well as ongoing creating presence in your absence activities.

▶ Here are the features within a sales-enablement platform that are needed to support virtual selling:

▷ Allows reps to quickly share digital content (documents and videos) with individual buyers (typically via email) *and* track how the content is being used.

▷ Allows reps (with two clicks) to generate videos of themselves talking to the buyer or using a voiceover PowerPoint presentation.

▷ Allows reps to create *interactive* content that goes above and beyond sending a trackable document or rep-generated video.

▷ Allows sellers to easily create individual digital sales rooms (DSRs) for each opportunity in their pipeline—to allow the buyer to experience a personalized, clutter-free, and efficient journey between the buyer and the seller.

▷ Allows the system to analyze *all* intelligence gathered from recorded calls, shared content, and digital sales room activities, as well as other information from your CRM system. It also allows the system to leverage AI to produce *actionable intelligence* to help make recommendations on what messaging to share, what content to share, and even what sellers may need to learn and improve!

Supporting Sales Teams with Modern Sales Enablement

▶ An overarching function that can mean success or failure in virtual selling is the sales-enablement function. At its core, sales enablement is the ongoing process of maximizing revenue per rep, by ensuring sellers convey the right concept using the right content throughout each stage of the buying process. A team-selling culture and dynamics are essential to success.

It's Time to Evolve Your Sales-Enablement Approach

▶ Five essential components of sales enablement:

▷ onboarding and training;

▷ launches and rollouts;

▷ content management;

▷ coaching and collaboration; and

▷ virtual selling.

Technology

▶ Four types of technology a sales manager should take advantage of to enable virtual selling:

▷ Modern learning technology: Modern learning technology allows managers to deliver formal courses, reinforcement learning, coaching, and just-in-time learning that ensure what's learned is retained and applied, resulting in true behavior change.

▷ Content management technology. This means: (a) reference material, YouTube-like video, how-tos, etc., (b) marketing collateral, and (c) "agile content" (short-shelf-life, time sensitive content relevant to sellers, often generated by the field, from trusted sources).

▷ Coaching technology: Coaching starts with knowing where and when sellers need improvement. There are several types of coaching that are essential:

☐ Self-coaching based on indicator or weaknesses identified;

☐ One-to-one managerial (or AI) coaches or dedicated trainers to provide feedback;

☐ "Coaching at scale"—where there are technology and processes to systematically identify which seller and which part (even down to which meeting recorded!) should be focused on to provide the all-important feedback to help a seller overcome challenges.

▷ Collaboration technology: There is power in asynchronous collaboration that can take place between a buyer and a seller backstage, free from the limitations of time and place. This asynchronous collaboration can also help teams collaborate internally more effectively.

The Takeaway from This Chapter:

▶ Executives and sales leaders should not be discouraged by the number of adjustments needed to pivot toward virtual selling as competitors are likely struggling as well.

CHAPTER 6: STEPPING CONFIDENTLY INTO THE FUTURE

▶ If you want to succeed in today's world, you must master the art of orchestration; learn to orchestrate the pieces that together will produce the results you want.

▶ Mastering virtual selling requires that you integrate both the frontstage and backstage areas of selling in order to create presence in your absence, making you a trusted advisor to the buyers and helping you achieve your desired outcome.

A Final Word on Mastery

▶ The definition of master that has informed our thinking in this book is "a person very skilled and able in some work, profession, science, etc.; expert."

▶ When you think about what masters have in common, they've all developed their mastery by doing something they loved over a long period of time. In addition, they all began as apprentices in one form or another.

▶ Clark Terry exemplifies both mastery and being a mentor.

▶ We can learn from children that there's joy in learning something new. Capturing a childlike curiosity and wonder is one of the secrets to becoming a master, understanding that it's the repetition of doing it over and over again that makes mastery a reality.

▶ As you move from apprenticeship to mastery, who you choose as your maestro makes a difference. Whether it is a peer, manager, or subject-matter experts, choosing the right master is important.

The Takeaway from This Chapter:

▶ The knowledge found in this book gives you the tools to become a master, but to truly succeed, you must practice dedication in your pursuit of learning.

There are three types of people in this world—those who make things happen, those who watch them happen, and those who wonder what happened. **Which kind will you be?**

Visit *masteringvirtualselling.com*

ABOUT THE AUTHORS

Yuchun Lee, CEO and co-founder of Allego,
has a proven business track record, serving as
CEO of marketing automation provider Unica,
guiding it through a successful IPO and sale to
IBM. Yuchun is also an executive in residence
at venture firm General Catalyst Partners, the
executive chairman of customer experience
software firm Clarabridge, board member of
Vertex Pharmaceuticals (NASDAQ: VRTX),
and an executive advisor with Summit Partners,
a global venture and private equity firm.

Mark Magnacca, President and co-founder of Allego, has an extensive background as a professional catalyst—bringing ideas and businesses to life. After starting a financial planning company right out of college and selling it a decade later, he then launched a sales consulting business to jump-start the digital transformation of many leading companies in the financial services industry. This work led to the founding of Allego. He's also the author of *So What? How to Communicate What Really Matters to Your Audience* and *The Product is YOU!*

Tony Jeary—The RESULTS Guy™—is a strategist, thought leader, and prolific author of 60+ titles, multiple best sellers, and hundreds of courses. Tony is unique and sought after by the world's best. His client list has now exceeded one thousand organizations in over fifty countries. He truly is a special resource that delivers and is a "secret weapon" to many business savvy leaders.

Tony lives and works in the Dallas/Fort Worth area, where at his brand-new think tank, the RESULTS Center, he and his handpicked team partner strategically plan and synergize teams, resulting in enhanced sales/profits and raising companies' value. Contact Tony at: *info@tonyjeary.com*